Landmark Vis

Anti

& Barbuda

Don Philpott

Acknowledgements

My sincere thanks go to all the people who helped me with research and assistance while writing this book. In particular I would like to thank the Antigua and Barbuda Department of Tourism, especially Karen Knowles and Dawn Anthony; Sandals Antigua Resort and Spa, American Airlines, Gabie Luery of Yepton Beach Resort and Robert Garzaroli of Jensen/Boga Inc.

Dedication

To Pam, my American Rose

Published by
Landmark Publishing
Ashbourne Hall, Cokayne Ave, Ashbourne,
Derbyshire, DE6 1EJ, England

Antigua

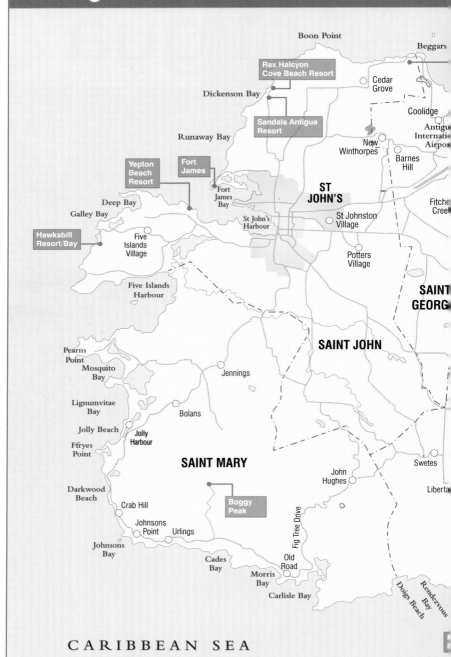

Boon Point

Beggars

Rex Halcyon Cove Beach Resort

Cedar Grove

Dickenson Bay

Coolidge

Sandals Antigua Resort

Antigu Internati Airpor

Runaway Bay

New Winthorpes

Barnes Hill

Yepton Beach Resort

Fort James

ST JOHN'S

Fort James Bay

Deep Bay

St John's Harbour

St Johnston Village

Fitche Cree

Galley Bay

Hawksbill Resort/Bay

Five Islands Village

Potters Village

SAINT GEORG

Five Islands Harbour

Pearns Point

Mosquito Bay

Jennings

SAINT JOHN

Lignumvitae Bay

Bolans

Jolly Beach

Jolly Harbour

Ffryes Point

SAINT MARY

John Hughes

Swetes

Darkwood Beach

Liberta

Crab Hill

Boggy Peak

Johnsons Point

Urlings

Fig Tree Drive

Johnsons Bay

Cades Bay

Old Road

Morris Bay

Carlisle Bay

Rendezvous Bay

Doigs Beach

CARIBBEAN SEA

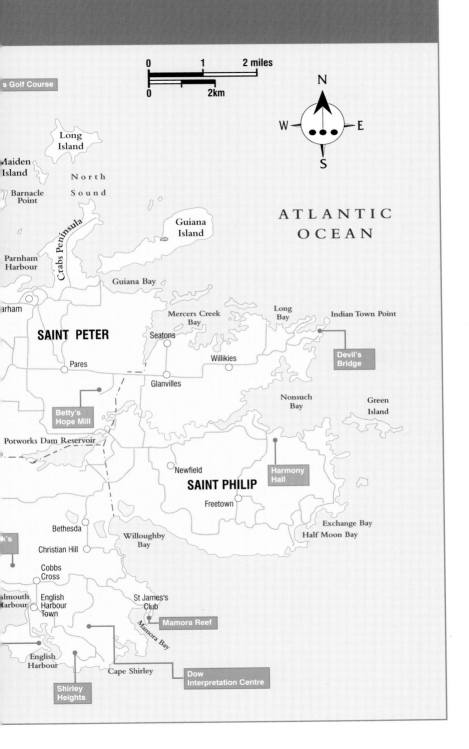

Contents

Index 95

Below: The sister Caribbean islands of Antigua and Barbuda are a top tropical destination, with 365 beaches, rainforests, and much more to explore. (Photo Credit: Antigua and Barbuda Ministry of Tourism)

The twin-island state of Antigua and Barbuda boasts some of the finest beaches in the Caribbean and superb year-round weather with high sunshine and low rainfall and humidity.

The waters offer world-class diving and sailing, and there is a wealth of other watersports. You can enjoy luxurious hotels and great restaurants and some of the freshest seafood you will ever taste. There are duty-free boutiques and crafts markets, laid-back beach bars, action-packed casinos, and historic sites and attractions. Above all, there are warm and friendly people waiting to make your trip one you will never forget.

Note: Antigua is pronounced as An-tee-gar.

When to Go

Many people feel that between November and April is the best time to visit because it is drier and cooler. Temperatures, however, do not vary a great deal throughout the year and any time is a good time to visit.

Getting there

By air

The VC Bird International Airport is 4 miles (6km) north-east of St John's, and is served by scheduled flights operated by a number of international carriers. There is a tourist information desk, duty-free shops, bank, post office, car rental agency, taxi rank, restaurants and bars. A 72-foot (22m) Observation Tower (82 steps) takes you to 252 feet (77m) above sea level for stunning views over the extensive airport expansion and surrounding coast. Always agree the taxi fare beforehand. Typical fares are US$11 to St John's, and US$31 to both Shirley Heights and Nelson's Dockyard.

From Europe

British Airways flies direct from London Gatwick (8 hours). Virgin Atlantic have twice-weekly direct flights. Caribbean Airlines offers a daily service via Barbados and Trinidad. There are also many charter flights during the summer. Many airlines fly to Miami and San Juan, Puerto Rico, where connecting flights can be taken to Antigua. Air France flies to Guadeloupe and KLM flies from Amsterdam to St Maarten, from where there are LIAT connections to Antigua.

From the US and Canada

Airline connections are offered by American Airlines through its Miami (3 hours) and San Juan (1 hour) hubs. Air Canada flies from Toronto and Continental Airlines flies from Newark and Baltimore (both 4 hours). There are also connecting flights via St Martin. Air Jamaica and Caribbean Sun also offer flights from the US and Puerto Rico to Antigua. Caribbean Airlines Flies daily from New York and Toronto to Trinidad.

Top Tips

Antigua has lots to offer all the family, top of the list being the 365 beaches. Here are some of Antigua's other top attractions.

Hiking

There are five easily walked trails in the Nelson's Dockyard National Park, up to one and a half miles (2.5 km) long through wooded valleys, past old fortifications and spectacular scenery and seascapes.

History

Visit the Admiral's House in Nelson's Dockyard and learn about pirates, sea battles and buried treasure.

Sugar

Visit Betty Hope, the only working sugar mill in the Caribbean. The children can learn how their favourite sugary snacks are made.

Wildlife

Spend a day at the Frigate Sanctuary on Barbuda – an unforgettable experience – plus see some of the other 170 species of birds.

Sea, sea, sea

Safe swimming and spectacular snorkelling – more than 2oo shipwrecks to explore. You can pet and feed stingrays at Stingray City on the north side of Antigua.

Family-friendly accommodation

Blue Waters – Supervised activities, beach games and room games.

Carllise Bay – Kids club, private cinema, teens area.

Jolly Beach Resort – Organised activities and games, traditional Caribbean story time and kids club clubhouse.

Jumbo Bay – Activities and games, outdoor children's centre.

St James Club – Kids club caters to younger guests aged 2–12 with lots of activities, games and nature walks.

From the Caribbean

LIAT operates scheduled services between Antigua and Anguilla, Barbados, Barbuda, Caracas, Carriacou, Dominican Republic, Dominica, Grenada, Guadeloupe, Guyana, Martinique, Montserrat, Nevis, Port of Spain, San Juan, St Lucia, St Maarten, St Thomas, St Vincent, Tortola and British Virgin Islands. Air St Kitts-Nevis, Carib Aviation and Norman

Local shop on Fig Tree Drive: Pineapples and More – Small, quaint fruit stands dot the countryside of Antigua and offer visitors a chance to taste delicious, native produce. (Photo Credit: Antigua and Barbuda Ministry of Tourism)

Nelson's Dockyard, located in English Harbour, is the only remaining example in the world of a British, Georgian naval dockyard. Here, holidaymakers can visit museums to learn about Antigua and Barbuda's unique history, and also explore the charming boutiques and art galleries that line the harbour. (Photo Credit: Antigua and Barbuda Ministry of Tourism)

Whether you are a water baby, landlubber or "all of the above", Antigua and Barbuda offers travellers many exciting adventures to choose from. (Photo Credit: Antigua and Barbuda Ministry of Tourism)

Aviation also operate from VC Bird International Airport, and offer charters to many islands close by. Caribbean Star Airlines operates scheduled services between Antigua, Anguilla, Barbados, Dominica, Grenada, Guyana, Nevis, St Kitts, St Lucia, St Maarten, St Vincent, Tortola, Trinidad and Tobago. Air Jamaica operates scheduled services between Antigua, Barbados, Jamaica and New York.

By sea

St John's has two ports, which serve visiting cruise ships — St John's Deep Water Harbour and the modern cruise ship facility at Heritage and Redcliffe Quay. Cruise ships also visit Nelson's Dockyard in English Harbour. Each year more than 300 cruise ships visit Antigua, together with thousands of yachts. Official points of entry are St John's, St James's Club, Falmouth Harbour and Jolly Beach Marina.

Cruise lines visiting Antigua include: Carnival, Celebrity, Cunard, Crystal, Disney, MSC, Norwegian, Oceania, Orient, Princess, Radisson, Royal Caribbean, Seabourne and Silversea.

Location and Landscape

The independent state of Antigua and Barbuda, together with its dependency of Redonda, lies in the north-eastern part of the Caribbean Sea and is part of the Leeward Islands, in the middle of the Lesser Antilles chain. To the west are the islands of Saba, St Eustatius, St Kitts and Nevis; to the south, the French island of Guadeloupe; and to the north, British Anguilla, French

Saint Barrhlemy and Dutch/French Saint Maarten/Saint Martin. Antigua is 295 miles (420km) south-south-east of Puerto Rico, and 1,300 miles (2,106km) south-east of Miami. The northern and eastern coasts of Antigua and Barbuda face the Atlantic Ocean, and the western and southern coasts face the Caribbean Sea.

Antigua

The island is 15 miles (24km) from east to west and 11 miles (18km) from north to the south at its widest. It covers 108 sq miles (280 sq km), and is the largest of the Leeward Islands. The island, consisting almost entirely of limestone coral, has a very indented coastline with many large deep-water bays and inlets offering safe anchorage, although the inshore waters off the north and north-east coasts can be treacherous due to reefs and shallows. The nature of the coastline gives rise to 365 sandy beaches, backed by gently rolling hills, often wooded or clad in lush flowering vegetation.

Christopher Columbus

Antigua was discovered by Christopher Columbus during his second voyage of exploration in 1493. He named the island after Santa Maria de la Antigua, the miracle-working patron saint of the cathedral in Seville, Spain, from whose port his expedition sailed. One of his three ships was named *Santa Maria*, the others being *Nina* and *Pinta*. After his death Columbus was buried in Seville Cathedral for a short time before being re-interred in the cathedral of Santo Domingo on Hispaniola.

Lying on the edge of the Caribbean plate the island is volcanic in origin, and was literally pushed above the surface of the sea by the pressure on the plate rim. It is generally low-lying with the highest land in the south-west. Boggy Peak at 1,330ft (405m) is the highest point. The island has no rivers and few springs. The main town is St John's, the capital.

Barbuda

Originally called Dulcina, Barbuda is 25 miles (40km) north of Antigua, 14 miles (23 km) from east to west, and 9.6 miles (15km) from north to south and covers an area of 62 sq miles (160 sq km). It is a wooded coral island with low hills and teems with wildlife. The highest point is Lindsay Hill at 143ft (44m) above sea level. There are no rivers or lakes on the island and the rainfall is less than on Antigua. The main settlement is Codrington.

Redonda

An uninhabited island rock 34 miles (55km) south-west of Antigua. It rises out of the sea to a height of 1,000ft (305m) and covers an area of 0.6 sq miles (1.6 sq km).

History

Long before the Spaniards arrived, the islands had been settled by several different groups of Amerindians – Siboney (or Ciboney), Taino, Arawak and Caribs – who had passed through the Caribbean from South America. There is evidence of Amerindian Siboney settlements dating back to 2000BC. The name Siboney comes from the Arawak word for 'cave-dweller', although many also preferred to live in small settlements close to the coast. They were Stone Age hunters and gatherers, and fashioned rough tools and weapons from stones and shells.

From the time of Christ, Arawaks started to arrive from nearby Caribbean islands to the south to escape the warlike Carib Indians. They named the island Wadaldi.

The Arawaks

The Arawaks were a peaceful people who grew basic crops like suchas, maize, inanioc and peppers. They also fished and foraged for food such as turtles and iguanas which were in plentiful supply. They lived in round, thatched 'hurricane-proof' huts in small villages ruled by a cacique (chieftain), and were skilled potters, weavers and boatbuilders. Their dug-out canoes were incredibly seaworthy, and their weaving skills were such that they could weave baskets from strips of palms that were totally watertight. The Arawaks slept in beds slung between two poles, and the hammock is one of their legacies. They worshipped gods of nature, represented by statues or idols made of wood, stone or bone.

The Caribs

The Arawaks were followed by the Caribs, who were feared warriors. Their battle canoes were powered by a hundred or more paddles and could, over a short distance, overhaul a sailing ship.

The original name of the Caribs was Kalina, meaning 'we alone are people'. The Spanish confused this with their word 'cariba', which was short for 'caribales' meaning cannibal, and this was then shortened to carib.

The Caribs were feared by early European explorers because of horrific stories about cannibalism, with victims being roasted alive on spits. They were even reported to have a taste preference, thinking Frenchmen were the most tasty, followed by the English and the Dutch, with the Spanish considered stringy and almost inedible.

Villages were built inland in forest clearings and huts had timber walls and thatched roofs. Early paintings show that the Caribs enjoyed dancing, either for pleasure or as part of rituals, and they played ball games. They were primarily fishermen and hunters, although they did cultivate kitchen gardens and developed a system of shift cultivation, known as conuco. They were also accomplished potters and weavers.

European occupation

The Spanish, having claimed ownership of the islands, then largely ignored them because of the hostile Indians and the lack of fresh water, and because there were much richer pickings further west on the islands of Cuba, Hispaniola and Puerto Rico.

Antigua was first settled by the English, from St Kitts, who landed in 1632 and claimed the island for the English crown. The settlers were attacked by the Caribs, but the Indians were no match for the well-armed English. The Caribs were either killed or enslaved or they fled, and the settlers cleared the land and planted tobacco, indigo and ginger. The island remained in English hands, although numerous attempts were made to take it by other foreign powers, especially the French and Spanish. In 1666 the French occupied the island for six months.

Barbuda

Barbuda was not settled until 1678. Seven years later the British crown deeded the island to the Codrington family, who used it to rear livestock and grow some cotton, the soil not being rich enough for sugar cane. There are many legends telling of the island's use as a slave farm, where the strongest, tallest slaves were used for breeding. It is possible that a slave farm was planned for Barbuda but there is no evidence that one ever existed, although some historians and anthropologists have suggested that it did, and this would account for the Barbudans being such a tall people.

Emancipation in 1834 hit the economy of the islands hard, and an earthquake in 1843 followed by a hurricane in 1847 caused further hardship. Although most of the plantations were near to ruin, sugar was the only crop the islanders knew how to produce – and the only occupation open to them – and it continued to be grown until well into the 20th century.

In 1860 Barbuda reverted to the British crown and was annexed by Antigua.

Late 19th century to the present

The Leeward Islands comprise of Anguilla, Antigua, Barbuda, Montserrat, St Kitts and Nevis, and in the late 19th century were governed by Britain as a single colony.

The islands remained part of the Leeward Islands Colony until this was broken up in 1956. In 1958 Antigua joined the West Indies Federation until it was dissolved in 1962. In February 1967, Antigua, led by former trade union leader Vere Cornwall Bird, became a State in Association with the United Kingdom with full control over its internal affairs, while Britain retained responsibility for external affairs and defending the islands.

The independence movement continued to gain support throughout the 1970s, although its leader, Prime Minister George Walter, was defeated in the 1976 elections by Vere Bird, who supported independence within a federation of adjacent islands. In 1978 Bird changed his position and petitioned the British Government for immediate independence. Negotiations were complicated by the fact that Barbuda wanted to secede from Antigua. Eventually Barbuda agreed to unite with Antigua as an autonomous state and, on 1 November 1981, the islands achieved their independence. Bird convinc-ingly won the 1984 elections. Bird's son, Lester, was elected as leader of the Labour Party when his father stepped down in 1994, and was Prime Minister until 2004 when Winston Baldwin Spencer, leader of the United Progressive Party, won the General Election. He is still Prime Minister.

Antigua's reputation as a tourist destination really started to grow during World War II when, under an agreement between the US and Britain, American forces were stationed on the island.

Climate

The near perfect year-round subtropical weather is one of the great attractions of Antigua and Barbuda. The sun nearly always shines and the two islands are among the driest in the Caribbean.

The average annual temperature is 79°F (26°C), with the average January and February temperatures – the 'coldest' months – about 77°F (25°C), and the average August temperature – the hottest month – around 82°F (27.5°C). Summer temperatures rarely rise above 90°F (32°C), and there is usually a welcoming onshore breeze.

Annual rainfall is about 40 inches (102cm). November is the wettest month, when about a quarter of the year's rain can fall, and showers are most frequent between September and December. It rains every month, but rarely for long, and downpours may be sudden and heavy, but then the sun comes back out again. Humidity is highest in April and May and between August and December, with November having the highest humidity due to the high rainfall.

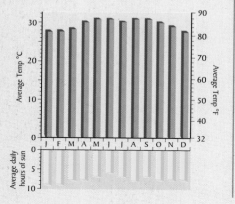

The sister Caribbean islands of Antigua and Barbuda boast 365 beautiful white and pink sand beaches, one for each day of the year. (Photo Credit: Antigua and Barbuda Ministry of Tourism)

The People

The islands have a population of about 70,000, of which about ninety per cent are of African descent, the rest being European and North Americans. Most people (36,000) live in St John's, the capital of Antigua, while Codrington, the main settlement on Barbuda, has a population of about 1,000.

Culture and Festivals

Carnival is the major annual festival. It commemorates the abolition of slavery on 1 August 1834, and is now one huge, exuberant jump-up. It was first held on 3 June 1952 as a one-day event as part of the Coronation celebrations for Queen Elizabeth II. Today, it takes place at the end of July and beginning of August and lasts for ten days with costume parades and lots and lots of partying and dancing. The Antigua Recreation Ground in St John's becomes a tented 'Carnival City' for the duration. In the calypso tents singers present their latest lyrics, always topical and often raunchy, and the Calypso King is crowned.

There are also musical offerings, food and drinks plus steel band competitions, the judging and crowning of the Carnival Queen, and a Caribbean Queens Competition. This is not a time for the faint-hearted, or those who like to take to their beds early, but it is a great festive occasion and one not to be missed, although you may well need a vacation afterwards to recover!

Antiguan music and dance features strong drum rhythms and is a lively mix of African and Caribbean. There are many excellent dance groups including the Obarala Performers and National Dance Group.

Antigua has also produced many fine artists, sculptors, potters and carvers such as Andrea Becker, Heather Doram, Jan Farara, Gilly Gobinet, Carl Henry, Sarah Fuller, Milton Henry, Michael and Imogen, Magrie Hunt, Luis Jarvis, Maria, Kinsella, Nick Maley, Cohn Martin, Nancy Nicholson, Priscilla Looby, Cadman Mathias, Freeston Williams, Gilly Bobinet, Chinwe Osaze and Gilly Huntington Rainey.

Hurricanes

Hurricane season lasts from June to November with September and October usually the busiest months for tropical storms. However, the last ten years have been more active than normal. The Government has detailed hurricane contingency plans, including evacuation and storm shelters. If a hurricane threatens the islands, follow the advice given locally.

Other main festivals

- International Cricket Week featuring the West Indies against visiting teams.
- Tennis Week is held in May at Currian Bluff Hotel and attracts top name seeds from the US and Europe.
- Antigua Classic Yacht Regatta takes place the week prior to Antigua Sailing Week in April. This regatta attracts classic wooden yachts of varying sizes from all over the world.
- Antigua Sailing Week takes place at the end of April and beginning of May at English Harbour. It attracts entries

from around the world for the racing, and provides an opportunity for near non-stop shore festivities.

- Carnival takes place the first Monday and Tuesday in August and is a vibrant summer festivity.
- Moods of Pan: an exciting showcase of concerts and workshops by International and Antiguan steel pan orchestras and musicians.

The Economy

Antigua's economy was originally based on agriculture, principally sugar cane, but tourism is now the major industry and income earner. Over 800,000 visitors arrive each year by air and sea.

There is some industry on Antigua producing clothing, paper goods, concrete blocks, beverages and some chemicals, and assembling electronic equipment. The soil on Barbuda was too poor to support sugar cane, and the land was used mostly for livestock farming, although some cotton was grown. The island's economy is now service-based with tourism and government services the two main employers.

The Government and Judiciary

Antigua and Barbuda is an independent state with a constitutional monarchy, with the British Queen Elizabeth II as the nominal head of state. She is represented on the island by the Governor-General. There is an elected seventeen-member House of Representatives and Senate, and executive power is in the hands of a Council of Ministers headed by the Prime Minister.

Flora and Fauna

The national flower is the Dagger Log (Agave Karatro), also called the Century Plant. The national fruit is the Antigua Black Pineapple.

The islands have lush tropical vegetation despite the low rainfall in places, and the overall impression is of greenery and stunning flowers. There are wonderful displays of flowering flamboyant (the Royal Poinciana), bougainvillea, hibiscus and frangipani.

Along the roads you can spot giant ferns and massive stands of towering bamboo, sugar cane, bananas, coconut groves, hanging breadfruit, mango, nutmeg, cocoa and pawpaw, and the most stunning array of spectacular-looking flowering plants from giant African tulip trees festooned with scarlet blossom, to tiny orchids.

Many homes have charming gardens with flowers, vegetables and trees. The trees are important for shade and also because many provide fruit. Bougainvillea flowers everywhere and there are scores of varieties of hibiscus, frangipani and poinsettia. There are heliconia, also known as the lobster plant, bird of paradise flowers and anthurium everywhere. The flamboyant tree is also known as the tourist tree because it bursts into red bloom during the summer.

In areas of lower rainfall the vegetation consists of thorn, cactus, yucca, mesquite and woodland. These plants are drought resistant and can survive in a dormant state, sometimes for months, after losing all their leaves because of lack of moisture. Along the coast you can find swamps, mangroves and marsh woodlands.

A note of Warning – the Manchineel

Found on many beaches, the Manchineel has a number of effective defensive mechanisms which can prove very painful. Trees vary from a few feet to more than 30 feet (10m) in height, and have widely spreading, deep forked boughs with small, dark green leaves and yellow stems, and fruit like small, green apples. If you examine the leaves carefully without touching them, you will notice a small pin-head sized raised dot at the junction of the leaf and leaf stalk. The apple-like fruit is very poisonous, and sap from the tree causes very painful blisters. It is so toxic that early Caribs are said to have dipped their arrow heads in it before hunting trips. Sap is released if a leaf or branch is broken, and even more so after rain. Avoid contact with the tree, don't sit under it, or a fallen branch, and do not eat the fruit. If you do get sap on your skin, run into the sea and wash it off as quickly as possible.

A young visitor to Antigua and Barbuda makes acquaintance with a baby sea turtle and one of its kin. Antigua's Environmental Awareness Group hosts turtle watches from late August to late October. The grandiose Hawksbill Sea Turtle has greatly influenced Antiguan culture and made the island its nesting ground thousands of years before Christopher Columbus set foot ashore. (Photo Credit: Antigua and Barbuda Ministry of Tourism)

Originally almost all of the island was covered by forest, but much of this was cleared to make way for the plantations. You can also spot mahogany and the white cedar as well as soursop, mango, coconut and breadfruit. Several species of orchid grow on the hillsides, many of them rare, and some so small that they can easily be overlooked. Close to the beach you can find red-barked turpentine trees and bearded figs.

Beach morning glory, with its array of pink flowers, is found on many beaches, and is important as its root system helps to prevent sand drift. The plant also produces nectar from glands in the base of its leaf stalks which attract ants, and it is thought this evolution has occurred so that the ants will discourage any leaf-nibbling predators. Other beach plants include seagrape and the manchineel, which should be treated with caution (see box above).

Ocean life

The sea teems with brilliantly marked fish and often even more spectacular-

Gazing over the clear, turquoise waters of Antigua and Barbuda from the balcony of one of many beachside resorts is the perfect start to any day. (Photo Credit: Antigua and Barbuda Ministry of Tourism)

looking coral and marine plants. Even if you just float upside down in the water with a face mask on you will be able to enjoy many of the beautiful underwater scenes, but the best way to see things is by scuba diving, snorkelling or taking a trip in a glass-bottomed boat.

There are scores of different corals, both hard and soft, that make up the reefs offshore. Only one, the fire coral, poses a threat to swimmers and divers because if touched it causes a stinging skin rash.

Among the more spectacular corals are deadman's fingers, stag-horn, brain coral and seafans, and there are also huge sea anemones and sponges.

Tropical fish species include the parrot fish, blue tang surgeon fish, tiny but aggressive damselfish, angelfish and wrasse.

Coastal swamps

A rich habitat for wildlife, with tiny tree crabs and burrowing edible land crabs which scurry around in the mud trapped in the roots of mangrove trees just above water level. Herons, egrets, pelicans and often frigate birds roost in the higher branches, while the mangrove cuckoo shares the lower branches with belted kingfishers.

Plants

Gardens are often full of flowers in bloom year-round, growing alongside exotic vegetables like yam, sweet potato and dasheen.

Flowering plants include the flamboyant tree, with its brilliant red flowers which burst into bloom in early summer, and long dark brown seed pods up to two feet long, which can be used as rattles when the seeds have dried out inside. Bougainvillea grows everywhere and seems to be in bloom year-round in a host of different shades. There are yellow and purple allamandas, poinsettia, hibiscus, anthurium and the ixora.

The leaves of the traveller's palm spread out like a giant open fan, the tree deriving its name from the belief that it pointed south to north, although it rarely does.

Along roadsides and hedgerows in the countryside, you can see the vine-like caralita, calabash with its gourd-like fruits, tamarind, and the distinctive star-shaped leaves of the castor bean, whose seeds when crushed yield castor oil.

Areas of scrubland have their own flora or fauna, with plants bursting into flower following the first heavy rains after the dry season. Century plants, with their prickly, sword-like leaves, grow for up to twenty years before flowering. The yellow flower stalk grows at a tremendous rate for several days and can reach 20 feet (6m) high, but having bloomed once, the whole plant then dies. Other typical scrubland vegetation includes aloe, acacia, prickly pear and several species of cactus.

Animals

There are few large animals but in the dense woodlands on Barbuda there are fallow deer and a few wild pigs. The islands do, however, have a rich population of mini-reptiles, insects, butterflies, moths (some of them huge) and many species of bats. There are also scorpion and large centipedes.

There are several species of endangered turtle – leatherback, hawksbill and green – and, offshore, dolphins, whales and manatees can be seen. The manatee is the animal which early mariners thought was a mermaid – obviously after having been at sea for too long, or having drunk too much local rum!

Birds

The islands have a rich birdlife with 170 species recorded as residents or visiting migrants.

Species include the Zenaida dove (also known as the mountain dove) and ground dove, hummingbirds, ani, kingbird, grackle, thrushie, aggressive pearl-eyed thrasher, herons, egrets, mocking bird, bananaquit, grassquit, smooth billed ani, Caribbean martin and the hovering American kestrel. The gentle cooing of the zenaida dove is a familiar island noise.

Offshore you may see tropic-birds and the magnificent frigate bird. It has a long black 7–8 foot (2–2.5m) wingspan, forked tail, and an apparent

The ani

A member of the cuckoo family, the ani is easily sighted by its dark plumage and parrot-like beak. It has a shrill squawing call, and strange and impractical nesting habits. The hen birds tend to lay their eggs in communal nests. The first bird lays her eggs, the second lays her eggs on top and so on. The birds take turns to sit on the eggs but the eggs at the bottom of the pile do not get enough body heat for incubation, so they rarely hatch.

effortless ability to glide on the winds. There are brown booby birds, named by sailors from the Spanish word for 'fool' because they were so easy to catch. Pelicans, which look so ungainly on land, yet are so acrobatic in the air, are common, as are laughing gulls and royal terns. Several species of sandpiper can usually be seen scurrying around at the water's edge.

Offshore islands have large bird populations, and on Great Bird Island you can see the red-billed tropic bird.

If you are really interested in bird-watching, pack a small pair of binoculars. Mini-binoculars are ideal for island birdwatching, because the light is normally so good that you will get a clear image despite the small object lens.

Fruits

As most of the plants, fruits, vegetables and spices will be new to the first-time visitor, the following brief descriptions are offered. A good place to learn more about the islands' fruits and vegetables is to visit one of the farmers' markets.

Banana

Bananas are one of the Caribbean's most important exports, thus their nickname 'green gold' – and they grow everywhere. On Antigua and Barbuda, banana trees are usually called fig trees!

There are three types of banana plant; the bananas that we normally buy in supermarkets originated in Malaya and were introduced into the Caribbean in the early 16th century by the Spanish. The large bananas, or plantains, originally came from southern India and the East Indies, and are largely used in cooking. They are often fried and served as an accompaniment to fish and meat. The third variety is the red banana, which is not grown commercially, and is quite rare.

Most banana plantations cover only a few acres and are worked by the owner or tenant, although there are still some very large holdings. A banana produces a crop about every nine months, and each cluster of flowers grows into a hand of bananas. A bunch can contain up to twenty hands of bananas, with each hand having up to 20 individual fruit.

Although they grow tall, bananas are not trees but herbaceous plants which die back each year. Once the plant has produced fruit, a shoot from the ground is cultivated to take its place, and the old plant dies.

Bananas need a lot of attention, and island farmers will tell you that there are not enough hours in a day to do everything that needs to be done. The crop needs feeding regularly, leaves need cutting back, and you will often see the fruit inside blue-tinted plastic containers, which protect it from insect and bird attack, and speed up maturation.

Breadfruit

Breadfruit was introduced to the Caribbean by Captain Bligh in 1793. He brought 1,200 breadfruit saplings from Tahiti aboard the *Providence*, and these were first planted in Jamaica and St Vincent, and then quickly spread throughout the islands. The slaves did not like them at first, but the tree spread and can now be found almost everywhere.

Breadfruit is a cheap carbohydrate-rich food, although pretty tasteless

The ocean awash with a golden glow marks the end of a perfect day in Antigua and Barbuda. (Photo Credit: Mark L. Craighead)

when boiled. It is best eaten fried, baked or roasted over charcoal. It is often used as a potato substitute, and makes excellent crisps (chips) when finely sliced and deep fried. It has large dark green leaves, and the large green fruits can weigh 10–12lbs (4.5–5.5kg). The falling fruits explode with a loud bang and splatter the pulpy contents over a large distance. It is said that no one goes hungry when the breadfruit is in season.

Calabash

Calabash trees are native to the Caribbean and have huge gourd-like fruits which are very versatile when dried and cleaned. They can be used as water containers and bowls, bailers for boats, and as lanterns. Juice from the pulp is boiled into a concentrated syrup and used to treat coughs and colds, and the fruit is said to have many other medicinal uses.

Cocoa

Cocoa is another important crop, and its Latin name *theobroma* means 'food of the gods'. A cocoa tree can produce several thousand flowers a year, but only a fraction of these will develop into seed-bearing pods. It is the heavy orange pods that hang from the cocoa tree which contain the beans which contain the seeds that produce cocoa and chocolate. The beans, containing a sweet, white sap that protects the seeds, are split open and kept in trays to ferment. This process takes up to eight days and the seeds must be kept at a regular temperature to ensure the right taste and aroma develops. The seeds are then dried.

In the old days people used to walk barefoot over the beans to polish them to enhance their appearance. Today, the beans are crushed to extract cocoa butter, and the remaining powder is cocoa.

Real chocolate is produced by mixing cocoa powder, cocoa butter and sugar. You can sometimes buy cocoa balls in the markets, which make a delicious drink. Each ball is the size of a large cherry. Simply dissolve the ball in a pan of boiling water, allow to simmer and then add sugar and milk or cream, for a rich chocolate drink. Each ball will make about four mugs of chocolate.

Coconut

Coconut palms are everywhere and should be treated with caution. Anyone who has heard the whoosh of a descending coconut, and leapt to safety, knows how scary the sound is. Those who did not hear the whoosh, presumably did not live to tell the tale. Actually, very few people do get injured by falling coconuts and that is a near miracle in view of the tens of thousands of palms all over the island, but it is not a good idea to picnic in a coconut grove!

Coconut trees are incredibly hardy and able to grow in sand even when regularly washed by salty seawater. They can also survive long periods without rain. Their huge leaves, up to 20 feet (6m) long in mature trees, drop down during dry spells so a smaller surface area is exposed to the sun, which reduces evaporation. Coconut palms can grow up to 80 feet (24m) tall, and produce up to 100 seeds a year. The seeds are the second largest in the plant kingdom, and these fall when ripe.

The coconut is the seed with its layer of coconut flesh surrounded by a hard shell. This shell is then surrounded by a layer of copra, a fibrous material, and this is covered by a large green husk. The seed and protective coverings can weigh 30lbs (13.5kg) and more.

The seed and casing are waterproof, droughtproof and able to float, and this explains why coconut palms, which

originated in the Pacific and Indian Oceans, are now found throughout the Caribbean – the seeds literally floated across the seas.

The coconut palm is extremely versatile. The leaves can be used as thatch for roofing, or cut into strips and woven into mats and baskets, while the husks yield coir, which is resistant to salt water and ideal for ropes and brushes and brooms. Green coconuts contain a delicious thirst-quenching 'milk', and the coconut 'meat' can be eaten raw, or baked in ovens for two days before being sent to processing plants where the oil is extracted. Coconut oil is used in cooking, soaps, synthetic rubber and even in hydraulic brake fluid.

As you drive around the island, you might see groups of men and women splitting the coconuts in half with machetes, preparing them for the ovens. You might also see halved coconut shells spaced out on the corrugated tin roofs of some homes. These are being dried before being sold to the copra processing plants.

Dasheen

Dasheen is one of the crops known as 'ground provisions' in the Caribbean, the others being sweet potatoes, yams, eddo and rannia.

The last two are close relatives of dasheen, and all are members of the aroid family, some of the world's oldest cultivated crops.

Dasheen, with its 'elephant ear' leaves, and eddo grow from a corm which when boiled thoroughly can be used like potato, and the young leaves of either are used to make calaloo (also spelled callaloo, kallaloo and several other ways). It is a spinach-like soup.

Mutiny on the *Bounty*

It was Captain Bligh's attempts to bring in young breadfruit trees that led to the mutiny on the *Bounty*. Bligh was given the command of the 215-ton *Bounty* in 1787 and was ordered to take the breadfruit trees from Tahiti to the West Indies, where they were to be used to provide cheap food for the slaves.

The ship had collected its cargo and had reached Tonga when the crew, under Fletcher Christian mutinied. The crew claimed that Bligh's regime was too tyrannical, and he and 18 members of the crew, who stayed loyal to him, were cast adrift in an open boat. The cargo of breadfruit was dumped overboard. Bligh, in a remarkable feat of seamanship, navigated the boat 3,600 miles (5,800km) until making landfall on Timor in the East Indies.

Some authorities have claimed that it was the breadfruit tree cargo that sparked the mutiny, as each morning hundreds of trees in their heavy containers had to be carried to deck, and then carried down into the hold at nightfall. It might have proved just too much for the already overworked crew.

Both dasheen and eddo are thought to have come from China or Japan but tannia is native to the Caribbean, and its roots can be boiled, baked or fried.

Guava

Guava is common throughout the West Indies, and the aromatic, sweet pink pulpy fruit is also sought after by birds, who then distribute its seeds.

The fruit-bearing shrub can be seen on roadsides and in gardens, and it is used to make a wide range of products from jelly to 'cheese', a paste made by mixing the fruit with sugar.

The fruit, which ranges from a golf ball to a tennis ball in size, is a rich source of vitamin A and contains more vitamin C than citrus fruit. Because it contains many small seeds, it is best eaten as a jelly or as ice cream, or drunk as juice. Guava juice is used as an ingredient in a number of tempting cocktails, but shouldn't be confused with the guavaberry, which also grows locally. The berries from this plant have been traditionally used by islanders to brew a special liqueur.

Mango

Mango can be delicious if somewhat messy to eat. It originally came from India and the East Indies, but is now grown throughout the Caribbean and found wherever there are people. Young mangoes can be stringy and unappealing, but ripe fruit from mature trees, which grow up to 50 feet (15m) and more, are usually delicious, and can be eaten raw or cooked. The juice is a great reviver in the morning, and the fruit is often used to make jams and other preserves, and great ice cream.

Nutmeg

Nutmeg trees are found on all the Caribbean islands. The tree thrives in hilly, wet areas and the fruit is the size of a small tomato. The outer husk, which splits open while still on the tree, is used to make the very popular nutmeg jelly. Inside, the seed is protected by a bright red casing which when dried and crushed produces the spice mace. Finally, the dark outer shell of the seed is broken open to reveal the nutmeg, which is dried and then ground into a powder, or sold whole so that it can be grated to add taste to dishes.

Passion fruit

Passion fruit is not widely grown but it can usually be bought at the market. The pulpy fruit contains hundreds of tiny seeds, and many people prefer to press the fruit and drink the juice. It is also commonly used in fruit salads, sherbets and ice creams.

Pawpaw

Pawpaw or papaya trees are also found throughout the islands and are commonly grown in gardens. The trees are prolific fruit producers but grow so quickly that the fruit soon becomes difficult to gather. The large, juicy melon-like fruits are eaten fresh, pulped for juice or used locally to make jams, preserves and ice cream. They are rich sources of vitamin A and C.

The leaves and fruit contain an enzyme which softens meat, and tough joints cooked wrapped in pawpaw leaves or covered in slices of fruit usually taste like much more expensive cuts. The same enzyme, papain, is also used in chewing gum, cosmetics, the tanning industry and, somehow, in making wool shrink-resistant. A tea made from unripe fruit is said to be good for lowering high blood pressure. Ripe papaya slices and lime make a delicious, healthy breakfast.

Pigeon peas

Pigeon peas are widely cultivated and can be found in many back gardens. The plants are very hardy and drought resistant, and produce prolific yields of peas which can be eaten fresh or dried and used in soups and stews.

Pineapples

Pineapples were certainly grown in the Caribbean by the time Columbus arrived, and were probably brought from South America by the Amerindians. The fruit is slightly smaller than the Pacific pineapple, but tastes more intense, especially if you have not tried a really fresh pineapple before.

Antigua's smaller 'black' pineapples are particularly succulent, and a prized export. Most fruit for export is picked before it is ripe so that it arrives many days later in reasonable condition. Really ripe fruit straight from the tree has an intense aroma, bursts with juice, and has almost no core, as this only develops as it ages.

Plantain

Plantain are another import from the East Indies and not to be confused with their cousins, the smaller yellow banana. Plantain are bigger, more versatile and a staple part of the Caribbean diet, and must always be cooked before eating.

One way of identifying bananas and plantain on the tree is that banana fingers on the hand generally point up, while plantain fingers normally point down, or so I am assured.

Other fruits

Soursop is a member of the same family as the sugar apple, and its spiny, pulpy

An Antiguan chef proudly shows off one of his culinary creations. Antiguan and Barbudan cuisine is first-class all the way, from casual to creative; West Indian zest melds with international fare to create a mélange of tastes for every palate. (Photo Credit: Antigua and Barbuda Ministry of Tourism)

fruits can be seen growing in hedgerows and gardens. They are eaten fresh, although they have lots of little black seeds, or are used for preserves, drinks and ice cream.

Sugar apple is a member of the annona fruit family, and grows wild and in gardens throughout the islands. It is also called the custard apple and sweetsop, because it is a lot sweeter than the soursop. The small, soft sugar apple can be peeled off in strips when ripe, and is like eating thick apple sauce. They are eaten fresh or used to make sherbet or drinks.

Sugar cane is still grown in gardens but not commercially. All of the cane grown to produce molasses for the rum industry is imported. The canes can grow up to 12 feet (3.5m) tall and, after cutring, the canes have to be crushed to extract the sugary juice. After extraction, the juice is boiled until the sugar crystals are formed. The mixture remaining is molasses and this is used to produce rum.

Food

Antigua offers a huge choice when it comes to eating out, from excellent traditional island fare to the finest international cuisine at the best tourist hotels.

Dining out offers the chance to experiment with all sorts of unusual spices, vegetables and fruits, with Creole and island dishes, and, of course, rum punches and other exotic cocktails.

Eating out is very relaxed and most restaurants do not have a strict dress code, although most people like to wear something a little smarter at dinner after a day on the beach or out sightseeing. Many hotels have a tendency to offer buffet dinners or barbecues, but even these can be interesting and tasty affairs.

Breakfast

Breakfast can be one of the most exciting meals of the day for a visitor. There is a huge range of fruit juices to choose from. Try a glass of watermelon juice, followed by a fresh grapefruit, or slices of chilled pawpaw or mango. Most hotels offer fruit plates containing a

The Tamarind

Originally from India, the tamarind is now a common sight throughout the Caribbean. The trees can grow very tall and bushy, and are long-living, with dangling bulbous pods that contain the rather tart fruit. The edible part is the pulp that surrounds the seeds, and it makes a delicious drink, and is also often added to curries and seasonings. It is also one of the special ingredients in Lea and Perrins Worcestershire Sauce which makes it so distinctive. It is even said that the pulp can be used to bring back the shine to tarnished brass and copper.

Quite often the area around the base of the tamarind is devoid of other vegetation, because the tree's roots give out a toxic chemical which kills off other plants.

wide choice, so you should be able to taste your way through them all during your stay.

The island's fruits also make great jams and preserves, and you can follow the fruit with piping hot roast spread with citrus marmalade or guava jam. Most tourist hotels also offer traditional American breakfasts for those who can't do without them.

During the summer there are fruits such as the kenip, plumrose, sugar apple and yellow plum. Green bananas and plantains are usually eaten raw, or boiled or steamed in the skin, then cut into slices and served very hot. They also make excellent chips when fried.

Starters

Starters include a huge choice of fruit juices from orange and grapefruit to the more unusual ones like soursop and tamarind. You can also drink green coconut 'milk'.

Traditional Caribbean starters also include dishes such as Christophene and coconut soup, and Callaloo soup made from the young leaves of dasheen or eddo, a spinach-like vegetable. The soup is made throughout the Caribbean and ochros, smoked meat and sometimes crab are added, as well as lots of herbs and spices. Chicken nuggets and marinated green bananas are also popular.

Fish and clam chowders are also popular starters. Try heart of palm, excellent fresh shrimps or scallops, smoked kingfish wrapped in crepes, or crab backs — succulent land crab meat sautéd with breadcrumbs and seasoning, and served re-stuffed in the shell. It is much sweeter than the meat of sea crabs.

Fish & seafood

The fish is generally excellent, and don't be alarmed if you see dolphin on the menu. It is not the protected species made famous by 'Flipper', but a solid, close-textured flat-faced fish called the dorado, which is delicious. Saltfish often appears on the menu. Salting was the most common form of preserving food, and allowed surplus catches to be kept safely until times of food shortage, or for when the seas were too rough for the fishing boats to go out.

Also available are snapper, grouper, kingfish, redfish, jacks, tuna, flying fish, lobster, swordfish, baby squid and mussels. There are delicious river crayfish and the larger saltwater variety, mussels and oyster.

Try seafood jambalaya – chunks of lobster, shrimps and ham served on a bed of braised seasoned rice; shrimp Creole – fresh shrimp sautéd in garlic butter and parsley and served with tomatoes; or fish Creole – fresh fish steaks cooked in a spicy onion, garlic and tomato sauce and served with rice and fried plantain.

Island 'fast food'

Island fast food includes parties, which are pastry cases stuffed with meats or saltfish, fritters and roti, which was brought to the islands by East Indian indentured workers in the 19th century. It consists of a thin dough wrapped around a hot spicy curry mixture containing beef, chicken, vegetables or fish. The chicken roti often contains small bones which some people like to chew on, so be warned.

For vegetarians there are excellent salads, stuffed breadfruit, callaloo bake, stuffed squash and pawpaw, and baked sweet potato and yam casserole.

Desserts

For dessert, try fresh fruit salad, with added cherry juice, and sometimes a little rum, a year-round popular dessert. There is a wide variety of fruit sherbets using tropical fruits such as soursop and tamarind.

Or try one of the exotic-tasting ice creams. There are also banana fritters and banana flambé, coconut cheesecake, and green papaya or guava shells simmered in heavy syrup.

Buffet

On the buffet table you will often see a dish called pepper pot. This is usually a hot, spicy meat and vegetable stew to which may be added small flour dumplings and shrimps. Pepperpot and fungee is the national dish. Fungee is a sort of dumpling made from cornmeal and okra.

There are also wonderful breads, and you should try them if you get the chance. There are banana and pumpkin breads, and delicious cakes such as coconut loaf cake, guava jelly cookies and rum cake.

Drinks

Rum is the Caribbean drink. There are almost as many rums in the West Indies as there are malt whiskies in Scotland, and there is an amazing variety of strength, hue and quality. The first West Indian rum was produced in the Danish Virgin Islands in the 1660s and by the end of the century there were thousands of distilleries throughout the Caribbean. Rum rapidly became an important commodity and figured prominently in the infamous Triangle Trade in which slaves from Africa were traded in Europe for rum in the West Indies which was sold to raise money to buy more slaves.

Rum has such fortifying powers that General George Washington insisted every soldier be given a daily tot, and a daily ration also became a tradition in the British Royal Navy, one that lasted from the 18th century until 1970.

Another note of warning - Pepper Sauce

On most tables you will find a bottle of pepper sauce. It usually contains a blend of several types of hot pepper, spices and vinegar, and should be treated cautiously. Try a little at first, before splashing it all over your food, as these sauces range from hot to unbearable.

If you want to make your own hot pepper sauce, take four ripe hot peppers, one teaspoon each of oil, ketchup and vinegar, and a pinch of salt, blend together into a liquid and bottle.

Columbus is credited with planting the first sugar cane in the Caribbean, on Hispaniola, during his third voyage, and the Spanish called the drink produced from it *aguardiente de cane*, although it was officially named as *saccharum*, from the Latin name for sugar cane. It was English sailors who abbreviated this name to rum. It is sometimes suggested that the word rum comes from an abbreviation of the word 'rumbullion'. While the origin of this word is unknown there is a record of it in 1672, and it was later used to describe a drunken brawl.

Rum can be produced in two ways. It can be distilled directly from the fermented juice of crushed sugar cane, or made from molasses, which is produced after the sugar, extracted from the cane by crushing, has been boiled until crystals form. Dark rums need keeping for many years in oak barrels, sometimes for up to 15 years. White rum is light-bodied and requires less time in the barrel.

The excellent English Harbour Rum is one of those distilled, blended and bottled on the island by The Antigua Distillery Ltd. They also produce the popular Cavalier range of rums. Rum shops are a popular feature of island life and there are usually one or two in each village. Like the English pub, they are focal points where people gather to have a drink, exchange gossip and play dominoes or warri. They are usually noisy places but don't confuse the raised voices with anger – people just have to shout in order to be heard. Rum shops also serve good, cheap local food, usually chicken and fresh fish.

Island beer is good, Wadadli being the most popular brew of the Antigua Brewery. The brewery began production in 1993, and the lager beer is named after the original Arawak word for the island. It is light and refreshing, and available both on tap and bottled.

Most tourist hotels and bars offer a wide range of cocktails, both alcoholic (usually very strong) and non-alcoholic. Tap water is safe to drink and mineral and bottled water is widely available, as are soft drinks.

Note: While many of the main tourist hotel restaurants offer excellent service, time does not have the same urgency as it does back home, and why should it after all, as you are on holiday. Relax, enjoy a drink, the company and the surroundings and don't worry if things take longer – the wait is generally worth it.

Island Tours

Such Great Heights – Visitors to Antigua can enjoy a breathtaking panoramic view of English Harbour from the hilltop of Shirle Heights. (Photo Credit: Mark L. Craighead

Getting around Antigua

By road

Antigua has almost 625 miles (1,000km) of roads and nearly all of the island is accessible, although conditions vary considerably. Many roads are not signposted at all even in towns, and some are unpaved. Great care needs to be taken off the main roads because of potholes and other surface damage and erosion. After heavy rains debris can also be washed onto the roads.

You can explore by rental car or taxi, and bicycles, which can be rented, also offer an excellent way to get around.

Taxis

Taxis are available at the VC Bird International Airport, most hotels, and in St John's. There are fixed taxi fares between the airport and most island destinations, and you can negotiate your own deals for excursions and tours. Fixed fares are posted at the airport. Always make sure when negotiating a taxi fare that you know which currency you dealing in – US$ or EC$: it could save an unpleasant situation later.

By bus

There are some bus routes operating to and from St John's, but they tend to run into St John's in the morning, and out of the capital late in the afternoon taking workers home. There are almost no services during the evening or on Sunday. The most regular service, and the most useful, is between St John's

and English Harbour. Buses leave the West Bus Station, which is on the waterfront off Valley Road and conveniently across from the Market, for the southern part of the island; and from the East Bus Station across from Independence Avenue by its junction with Factory Road, for the north and eastern parts. Exploring by bus is a great way of getting around and meeting the islanders, and it is also cheap.

By air

LIAT, the regional airline, flies between Antigua and twenty-five Caribbean islands, and schedules are timed so that day trips are possible. Carib Aviation, a charter company based at VC Bird International Airport, also offers day tours in addition to its regular charter flights.

By sea

There are several boats offering trips to Barbuda, and yachts are available for charter, either crewed or bareboard for exploring offshore islands and secluded bays. You can also charter a boat to visit the bird island of Redonda.

St John's

The island capital is one of the oldest trading ports in the Caribbean with a 300-year history. It still has many historic buildings, although most of these date from the last 150 years. Earlier buildings, constructed of wood, were destroyed over the centuries either by fire or by hurricanes and earthquakes.

Walking tour

The capital is easy to get around by foot as it is laid out in a grid, a legacy of the many natural disasters which allowed the town planners to rebuild from scratch. Driving, however, can be a problem until you get used to the one-way system. If you remember that streets run parallel with each other and you can't turn into the one you want, simply follow the one way system round the block to gain access.

While some modern concrete structures have gone up, the town retains its charm through its fine old wooden and stone buildings, many brightly painted in pastels, and their overhanging balconies and shutters. Traditionally, town homes would have a stone-built ground floor with a wooden storey above.

There are the up-market shopping complexes at Heritage Quay and Redcliffe Quay, but also many other types of stores to be visited on the streets in from the waterfront. To the south is the old market where island fruits and vegetables are sold, and along the waterfront on the outskirts of town fishing boats are hauled up on the beach, while the fishermen repair their nets and sell their catches. The Woods Centre is a shopping area on the Friar's Hill Road on the outskirts of St John's, comprising supermarkets, stores, banks, pharmacy, beauty salon, restaurants and a food court. It is open daily until 10pm.

Most of the main sights, however, are in St John's, close to the waterfront, and contained within a few blocks.

The Tourist Information Office is on

The Botanic Gardens

The Gardens were first opened in 1888 and moved to their present site, close to the Parliament Building, five years later.

The site originally covered 8 acres (3 hectares) and was used by the Government for agricultural research into plants that were grown commercially. The gardens closed in 1950 and quickly became overgrown, but at the end of the 1980s a committee was set up to restore them, and now you can enjoy their work. The garden has a wide range of plants found on the island and has rich bird and animal life too.

the corner of Thames and High Streets, where you can find out what is going on and if there are any special events taking place. The Post Office is a short step away towards the waterfront, and the Cenotaph, which commemorates those Antiguans who died during the two world wars, stands at the top of the High Street. At the other end is the Westerby Memorial, erected in 1892 in memory of Bishop George Westerby and his Moravian missionaries. Between the Post Office and the Old Administration Building is the VC Bird Monument, in memory of Dr Vere Cornwall Bird, the first Premier. It was unveiled in 1987.

Antigua is one of the most popular cruise ship destinations in the Caribbean and most ships arrive at the modern Cruise Ship Dock. The ships are then able to disgorge their passengers straight into the heart of the town through Heritage Quay, a relatively new tourist development close to the Cruise Ship Dock with information desk, the Heritage Hotel, more than 40 duty-free shops, restaurant and casino.

King's Casino is the largest casino on the island with nightly gambling and entertainment. The casino features The King Machine, the world's largest slot machine, and a sports lounge with four televisions and a 10-foot (3m) screen. It is open Monday to Saturday from 10am to 4am, and on Sunday from 6pm to 4am ☎ 462-1727.

Further south is the West Bus Station where you can catch buses to the south of the island and English Harbour. The Market is at the junction of Valley Road and All Saints Road, and always worth a visit not just for the sheer vibrancy, but also for the chance to haggle over delicious fruits. On sale is a huge array of island produce from fruits and vegetables to exotics herbs and spices. At the end of All Saints Road is the *Industrial School for the Blind*, a workshop where you can see the skilled weavers at work and buy their products ☎ 462-0663. From the Market, head back into town, then turn right onto New Street and cross over to the Queen Elizabeth Highway. On your right is the Holy Family Cathedral, and on your left, the Government Administration Buildings.

Return to Independence Avenue and turn right with Country Pond on your left. Further along is the East Bus Station across the junction on your

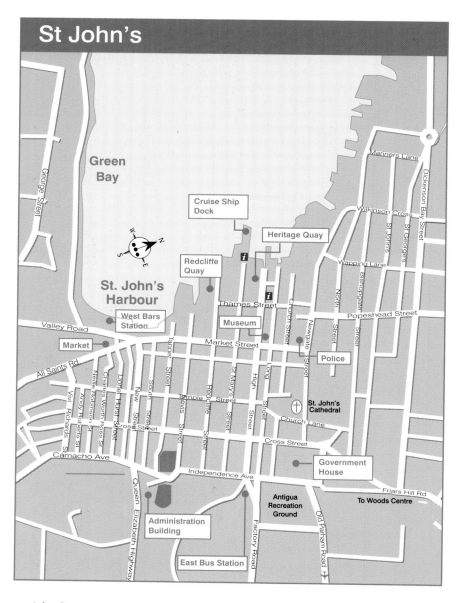

St John's

right, then you pass the Antigua Recreation Ground on your left, and Government House on your left. **Government House** was originally two buildings but they were joined and considerably extended. It is noted for its impressive two-floor colonnade and striking early 19th-century interior. Tours are by appointment only. ☎ 462-0003.

Return to Long Street and turn left and then left again into Church Street and the Anglican **St John's Cathedral**

St John's Cathedral

Built originally in wood between 1681 and 1683, the Cathedral was rebuilt in stone between 1742 and 1745 but destroyed by a massive earthquake almost a century later in 1843. The cornerstone of the present building was laid in 1845. The Cathedral, having been elevated to that status in 1842, was consecrated in 1848.

The stone cathedral with its twin towers has an unusual interior – it is encased in wood, designed to protect it from both earthquake and hurricane, and this has obviously been successful, as it has withstood both many times since. The two statues at the south entrance of the Cathedral are of St John the Baptist and St John the Apostle. They were sculpted in the eighteenth century and were bound for Dominica, then controlled by the French, aboard a ship that was captured by a British Royal Navy vessel. The 'liberated' statues were brought to Antigua and later presented to the Cathedral.

St. John's Cathedral is visible from Antigua's capital, is regarded as a national monument. (Photo Credit: Antigua and Barbuda Ministry of Tourism)

In Antigua and Barbuda, visitors can escape the hustle and bustle of everyday life. Some on-island spas offer yoga classes to inspire peace and help guests achieve relaxation nirvana. (Photo Credit: Antigua and Barbuda Ministry of Tourism)

Shopping

Market Day

Saturday is Market Day in St John's and this is the place to be if you really want to shop with the locals. Although the market is at the southern end of Market Street, stalls are set up all around town. If you are self-catering, this is the best place to buy fruit and vegetables and engage in some friendly bartering. Local handicrafts are also sold. If you want fresh fish just stroll down to the harbour area behind King's Casino and negotiate a price with the fishermen as they return with the day's catch.

Heritage Quay offers world-class shopping at bargain prices, with top name stores and boutiques selling a wide range of goods from clothing to leather goods and arts and crafts. It is the only duty-free shopping area on Antigua and as it is close to the cruise ship dock it gets very crowded when a ship is in port. At other times, it is a pleasant place to stroll around, window-shop, perhaps watch a street performer and enjoy a drink or meal at one of the watering holes. It also has public restrooms. This is a great place to shop if you are interested in jewelery, especially tanzanite. You can also purchase the finest Cuban cigars, which Americans can enjoy during their island visit as it is illegal to import them into the US.

Redcliffe Quay is a short walk to the south along the Harbour. It is a delightful historic waterfront area with well-restored nineteenth century buildings and warehouses now the home of shops, boutiques, bars and restaurants. It is a fun place to explore with narrow alleys and tucked away shaded courtyards draped with colourful tropical foliage. The Quay has a wide range of shops selling everything from clothing to videos and toys. Visit Kate Design, which exhibits the work of artist Kate Spencer that ranges from oils and watercolours to table mats, scarves and jewelery. All her work is inspired by the people and scenery of the Caribbean. There are several boutiques selling island-designed clothing, batik and handicrafts.

The Woods Center, off Friars Hill Road, on the outskirts of St John's, is the island's newest shopping mall and boasts The Epicurean, Antigua's most modern supermarket, as well as a drugstore, post office, dry cleaners and many other stores. It is also the home of Get Physical, a state of the art fitness centre and a bookshop.

St Mary Street also has a number of interesting shops, many of them catering to locals rather than tourists, but there are bargains to be had. The Map Shop has books on local and Caribbean history, culture, flora and fauna.

(see box on p.35). Continue along Church Street and then turn right into Market Street past the police station on the corner. This used to be a munitions store and nearby is the old guardhouse and the island's first jail.

Cross over Church Street and visit **The National Museum of Antigua and Barbuda**, on the corner of Market and Long Streets. It is in the Old Court House, the oldest building still in use in the capital. Designed by Peter Harrison, it was started in 1747 and opened three years later, but has had to be rebuilt a number of times because of natural disaster damage. The building was constructed of yellow free stone quarried on Long Island, Guana Island and Pelican Island. The court was on the ground floor and the Council and Assembly met upstairs. Although the building and exhibits are historic, the museum's approach to learning is not. The museum was opened in 1985 and is now a popular educational and research facility, with a fine library and National Archives. The museum traces the island's history from pre-Columbian times to independence, and many of the exhibits encourage a 'hands-on' approach with 'please touch' signs aimed especially at children. There are displays about the island's geology, a life-size Arawak hut, a working 1829 steam engine once used to cut sugar cane, and a model of a sugar plantation. On display is the cricket bat used by Viv Richards to score the fastest ever test century – off 56 balls in St John's, in April 1986. A container full of pieces of broken seventeenth-century china invites you to try to put all the pieces to-gether. The museum has a calendar

of regularly changing special exhibits and is also the home of the Historical and Archaeological Society and the Environmental Awareness Group. There is a small gift shop which is open Monday to Thursday from 10am to 3pm, Friday 8.30am to 3pm and on Saturday from 10am to 1pm ☎ 462-1469. Admission is free but donations are appreciated.

Island Tours

While nearly all of Antigua can be reached by car, either on main or secondary roads, it is often necessary to retrace your route a small distance in order to continue with your tour. There are lots of side roads to explore and with 365 beaches around the island, you can usually get one all to yourself. Don't drive too fast because most road junctions are not marked. If you overshoot your road, drive on and turn round when safe to do so. If you get lost, simply ask an islander.

Tour 1 – The South

Head south out of St John's and then follow the road which runs south of the Harbour to Five Islands, a peninsula with a number of hotels and fine beaches. It is not easy to find the road as there are few signposts, but you turn by the King George Playing Fields. The road runs through the shanty town suburbs of St John's. Once you are out in open country the first main turning on your right heads for the sea and on top of Goat Hill are the remains of **Fort Barrington**, built, like Fort James, to protect St John's Harbour as well as Deep Bay to the east. The best way to reach the fort is from the track which

Nelson's Dockyard, located in English Harbour. (Photo Credit: Antigua and Barbuda Ministry of Tourism)

Antigua and Barbuda offers travelers many exciting adventures to choose from. (Photo Credit: Antigua and Barbuda Ministry of Tourism)

The gorgeous crystal clear, turquoise waters and lush, green landscape of Antigua and Barbuda set the stage for romance. (Photo Credit: Antigua and Barbuda Ministry of Tourism)

runs up the hill from the northern end of Deep Bay.

Deep Bay is a popular beach and dive site. The star attraction is the wreck of the freighter **Andes**, which sank in the mouth of the bay in 1907, and lies in just 20 feet (6m) of water.

Retrace your route back to the main road then drive south through Golden Grove and Ebeneezer. Cedar Hall and Green Castle Hill are on your left as you drive on to Jennings. There are a number of megaliths on top of the 565-foot (172m) high Greencastle

Watersports in Antigua and Barbuda. (Photo Credit: Antigua and Barbuda Ministry of Tourism)

Fort Barrington

This fort has seen more action than any other on the island. It is not known when the original structure was built, but in 1652 Prince Rupert and Royalist forces captured the fort and used the cannon to sink one ship anchored in Deep Bay and force the surrender of a second. In 1666 the French attacked the island and captured the fort, but were forced to return it to the English in 1677.

The present fort dates from 1779–80 and was named in memory of Admiral Barrington who, a year earlier, had defeated the French at the Battle of Cul de Sac which restored St Lucia back to the British.

There is a plaque in memory of William Burt, who was Governor when the fort was built. He is recorded as 'Emperor and Governor of the Leeward Islands'. The fort served as a signal station until 1960.

Hill, which is an old volcano. There are excellent panoramic views from the summit. Many side trips can be taken along this route, such as the short detour west to Mosquito Cove and Pearns Point.

There are many beautiful beaches along this south-western stretch of coastline, and while they are not all easy to reach, the effort is always worthwhile.

The road then cuts closer to the coast at Lignumvitae Bay, named after the hardwood that used to grow just inland from there. Today the bay has hotels, restaurants and shops and is a popular tourist beach.

Jolly Harbour Marina and Shopping Centre, at Lignumvitae Bay, offers the opportunity for souvenir shopping with restaurants and bars to sustain you before, during and after. It is the home of the Jolly Harbour Yacht Club and the Carib Cup Regatta. Shops offer a wide range of goods from beach wear to arts and crafts, and curios from around the world to the latest electri-cal gadgetry. There are berths for 130 yachts, also ships' chandlers, a tackle and bait shop and boat repair yards. There are also waterfront restauranrs, bars and a casino.

Excavations at Jolly Harbour have found a settlement dating back to 1775.

Follow the coast road round through Crab Hill to Johnsons Point on the south-west corner of the island, where there are the remains of an eighteenth, century fort. Inland are the Shekerley Mountains, the highest hills on the island, with Boggy Peak the highest point. A short way beyond Urlings is Brooks Old Mill, just inland from Cades Bay, and the road then runs on to Old Road. There is a small road inland from Cades Bay which allows access to Boggy Peak, and the climb to the summit is worth it for the stunning views. On a day free from heat-haze you can usually see Guadeloupe to the south and St Kitts to the north.

Old Road was the site of the first English settlement on Antigua and the fort was built to protect Carlisle Bay. Many place names include the word 'road', which is an old nautical term for a safe anchorage.

Climbing up the hill you come to the village of John Hughes, where you can park and take the nature trail which leads through the Wallings Forest of deciduous trees to a Victorian dam and reservoir about half a mile (0.8km) away. The dam took three years to build and was completed in 1893.

To the south-east of Liberta, and to the east of the road, is Monk's Hill, on top of which are the ruins of **Fort George**. You can reach the fort by taking the side road to the village of Table Hill Gordon. From there it is about a mile (1.6km) to the fort. If you do not have a four-wheel-drive vehicle you will have to walk there and back. The hill is named after General Monk, Duke of Albemarle, and although known as Monk's Hill fort, its original name was Great George Fort, after the English patron saint.

The road then runs south into Falmouth, one of the coastal communities that falls within the 15-square-mile (39sq km) national park area which also encompasses Nelson's Dockyard, English Harbour and Shirley Heights. Other communities within the park are English Harbour and Cobbs Cross, which is why the national park is also called The Living Park.

Fort Charles on Blake Island in Falmouth Harbour is one of the oldest forts on Antigua. It was built in 1672 and extended in 1714 when it had a battery of fourteen cannon.

Cobbs Cross is noted for its egret colony, and flights of these graceful white birds make spectacular sunrises and sunsets even more stunning.

English Harbour Town is separated from Falmouth by a small neck of land. English Harbour is even more protected than Falmouth Harbour, and this was quickly appreciated by the Royal Navy, who chose it as a site for a naval dockyard. It had many advantages: it

Fig Tree Drive

This is an ancient road that runs from Old Road, at the head of Carlisie Bay, inland round Signal Hill and Sugar Loaf Hill, before turning south at Swetes for Liberta. It winds its way inland through the steep-sided, densely wooded hills covered in lush tropical vegetation. This was one of the island's main sugar cane growing areas, as evidenced by the many old sugar mills along the way.

There are also several pretty churches, an indicator of how large the area's population must have been in the late 18th and 19th centuries. The most spectacular of these churches is the pink **Tyell's Roman Catholic Church** on the main road just north of the Swetes junction. The drive is very pretty, although the road is a bit rough in places, and it gets its name from the banana trees along the way, known locally as fig trees. You can also see guava, mango and coconut.

Island Forts

For much of its early life Antigua was surrounded by hostile European powers and the island was attacked by French, Spanish and Dutch pirates. When war broke out between the European powers it usually resulted in conflict in the Caribbean as their respective navies fought it out in the offshore waters.

Because of its strategic importance, a ring of forts was built in the seventeenth and eighteenth centuries to protect the island, its busy quays and the hugely profitable sugar crop.

More than 40 forts were built, some of them huge constructions covering many acres and taking a decade or more to fininsh. In an offical report in 1734, Goveror William Matthews listed 27 manned forts around the island with a total of 133 cannon. The largest was Fort George with 33 cannon, followed by Fort James with 16, Fort Berkeley with 12 and Fort Charles with 10. Many of the forts were little more than small gun emplacements with just one or two cannon, and few ever had to fire their cannon in action.

Following Britain's defeat of France and the end of the Napoleonic Wars, the French no longer posed a threat in the Caribbean and the forts were gradually run down. Luckily, some survive, albeit as ruins, and can still be visited. Some of the cannon remain in place, but most of the weaponry has long since been removed, and either sold as scrap or incorporated into the island's landscape as traffic bollards.

Main forts

Codrington	Dow's Hill	Fort Barrington
Fort Berkeley	Fort James	Fort George
Fort Shirley		

Lesser forts

Dickenson Bay	Falmouth	Fort Byam
Fort Charles	Fort Isaac	Fort William
Hamilton Point	Hawk's Nest	High Point
Mercer's Creek	Old Road Fort	

To learn more about the forts, visit the National Museum in St John's.

Fort James was built in 1703 by the British to protect the northern entrance of Antigua's St John's Harbour. (Photo Credit: Antigua and Barbuda Ministry of Tourism)

Inside Nelson's Dockyard. (Photo Credit: Antigua and Barbuda Ministry of Tourism)

Falmouth Harbour

Falmouth Harbour has provided safe anchorage for more than 400 years, and Falmouth is one of the island's oldest settlements. Work on the fortifications to defend the Harbour to the south started in 1669. The fort was huge, covering an area of 7 acres (3 hectares), and took 16 years to complete.

The tall perimeter walls survive largely intact. Inside are the ruins of many of the old military buildings and structures, including cisterns for storing precious water supplies, and the magazines for holding the powder for the battery of 32 cannon. Nowadays the Harbour is as busy as ever, catering for charter vessels and yachts from around the world.

offered a safe, deep water anchorage, the headlands protected sheltering vessels from hurricanes, and the Harbour and approaches could be easily defended.

These forts included **Fort Berkeley**, built to protect the western approaches. The fort was started in 1704 and extended and strengthened on several occasions over the next fifty years. It eventually had twenty-nine cannon. A nature trail leads to the Fort.

Nelson's Dockyard

Nelson's Dockyard is one of the most historic dockyards in the world, and one of the safest. Over the centuries it has been used by pirates and privateers, and during the Napoleonic Wars it provided a safe haven for British Royal Navy ships when they were not harassing French vessels. Work on the

dockyard started in 1743 and continued for almost a hundred years as more refinements were added until it became one of the most important naval bases in the Caribbean, and the headquarters of the Royal Navy's powerful East Caribbean fleet.

Over the years, the dockyard has played host to some of Britain's most famous seafarers, including Admirals (Horatio) Nelson, Rodney and Hood. Admiral Lord Rodney is famous for his victory over the French fleet under de Grasse off Dominica during the American Revolution; Admiral Viscount Samuel Hood was a brilliant naval strategist who thwarted the French invasion of British St Kitts and Nevis, and later blockaded most of the French navy inside their base at Toulon in the Mediterranean for four months.

Nelson's Dockyard is now important as the world's last Georgian dockyard, and is protected as part of a national park area, although the Harbour and year-round marina now teems with luxury yachts rather than fighting ships. The eighteenth-century quay and its buildings have been well restored and the area can have changed little over the last 200 years.

The stone warehouses, boathouses, blacksmith's, sawpits, sail loft with its massive pillars which took 15 months to build and garrison quarters are now home to shops, boutiques, inns and restaurants. The Officers' Quarters is built over a massive underground cistern which stored water. Officers lived in the building while their ships lay at anchor during the hurricane season. There is now an art gallery upstairs.

The original Copper and Lumber

Dow's Hill

Dow's Hill overlooks English Harbour and is the home of the new **International Centre** ☎ 481-5045. There are great views from the hilltop over the sites of the first European settlements established in the early 17th century, and the fortifications around English Harbour.

The Centre, named after General Alexander Dow, who commanded the Shirley Heights garrison, has been cleverly built incorporating old fortifications. The Centre's highlift is a multi-media presentation called Reflections of the Sun. The presentation has been designed so that you view the first Amerindian settlers, through the Plantocracy, the British military period and the freedom struggle to Emancipation and beyond.

The nearby **Belvedere** is built on what remains of the 18th-century Governor-General's residence. The house was destroyed by an earthquake in 1843 although its foundations and those of the outbuildings can still be seen. From its breathtaking vantage point the belvedere offers true panoramic views, and interpretative panels help you pick out important landmarks.

Also on Dow's Hill is the entrance to the **Batcave**. It is on the campus of the medical school, and there are tours of the cave accompanied by a fascinating discourse on island folklore. According to legend there is an undersea tunnel running from the cave all the way to Guadeloupe, and this was supposedly used as an escape route by runaway slaves.

Store, with its unique Georgian arched courtyard, is now a delightful hotel. Originally copper was beaten onto the hulls of wooden ships to strengthen them, while the timber was needed for repairs. The huge stone bollards that were used to moor the men-o'-war, still stand proudly along the water's edge.

The dockyard's main purpose was to act as a careening station for vessels. The ships' bottoms would be covered in barnacles and scratches after crossing the Atlantic. Having reached the shelter of the quay, the ships would be pulled onto their sides using ropes attached to massive capstans, so that the sailors could clean the exposed bottom and repaint and repair them. The capstans have been restored and stand at the water's edge.

The **Admiral's House**, where Nelson stayed briefly in 1805 while senior captain, is now the dockyard Museum with exhibits chronicling the history and work of the dockyard, and some of its famous visitors. Despite its name, there is no evidence that any admiral ever lived in the house. By the museum stands an old sandbox tree which is at least 200 years old. It derives its name from the large pods filled with sand which the officers kept on their desks to sprinkle over wet ink to help it dry. Behind the building is the old stone

Blockhouse Hill

Situated on Cape Shirley, over 400 feet (122m) above the sea, Blockhouse Hill derives its name from the fortified structures built on the crest.

These include gun emplacements, power stores, water cisterns and barracks, and the blockhouse, built in 1787. It was designed as the place for last resistance in case of attack, but was largely used as officers' quarters.

Close by is the old military cemetery, which has an obelisk commemorating soldiers of the 54th Regiment who died during a yellow fever outbreak between 1848 and 1851. The Shirley Heights garrison was withdrawn in 1854 when the troops were dispatched to fight in the Crimea, and it was never manned again.

kitchen and the ancient ovens are still in use by the bakery.

Clarence House was built in 1787 on the hillside opposite the dockyard, and this was where Prince William Henry, Duke of Clarence and captain of the HMS *Pegasus*, stayed when in dock. A close friend of Nelson, a fellow captain, he later became King William IV, and other members of

Below: Sail Away – the island of Antigua is home to some of the greatest sailing and races in the Caribbean. Speeding along the open waters of Antigua, even the most stressed out vacationers will feel invigorated. Antigua's Sailing Week is only one of the many opportunities to hop onboard a sailing boat, catamaraning or yacht and let the trade winds carry you along. (Photo Credit: Antigua and Barbuda Ministry of Tourism)

Visitors can tee off at one of three golf courses in Antigua and Barbuda. (Photo Credit: Antigua and Barbuda Ministry of Tourism)

The clear, turquoise waters and rolling hillsides of Antigua and Barbuda make it one of the world's top tropical destinations. (Photo Credit: Antigua and Barbuda Ministry of Tourism)

the British Royal Family have since been guests there. Clarence House is now the official country home of the Governor-General. When he is not in residence, this Georgian house, complete with period furnishings, is open to the public.

The dockyard played a vital strategic role in Britain's retaining her Caribbean colonies during the nineteenth century, but as European nations made peace there was less need for a strong naval presence in the Caribbean.

Emancipation and the extensive use of sugar beet in Europe also hit the profitability of the sugar cane plantations, so the need to protect this trade diminished. These two factors brought about the demise of the dockyard and it was closed in 1889.

The area fell into disrepair, but in 1951 an adventurous restoration agenda was initiated as part of a joint scheme between the Antigua and Barbuda National Parks Authority and the Canadian International Development Agency, and ten years later it re-opened rather ironically as Nelson's Dockyard. Although Nelson spent three years based at or sailing from the dockyard, he was not overly fond of it, and described it variously in his diaries and letters as 'this vile spot' and 'this barbarous island'. He was stationed at the dockyard between 1784 and 1787 as Captain of the frigate HMS *Boreas* and his disillusionment with Antigua was due in part of his having to enforce the Navigation Act, which outlawed the islanders' lucrative trade with passing American ships. The Act also annoyed the British colonial officers on the island who had turned a blind eye to

the trade and profited from it.

While based on Antigua, however, Nelson met Frances 'Fanny' Nesbit, a young widow from nearby St Kitts. He met her in March 1785 and married her on Nevis two years later, returning to England with her and her young son immediately afterwards. Prince William Henry acted as best man. Nelson returned to the dockyard briefly in 1805 as Admiral in charge of the British fleet chasing the French, a confrontation which ended in both his victory and death at the Battle of Trafalgar, off the Spanish coast on 21 October of that year.

Today Nelson's Dockyard and the surrounding park is delightful, and makes a fascinating visit. There is a Visitors' Centre (☎ 460-1379) plus shops and boutiques, hotels and restaurants – and nearby, of course, beautiful beaches.

It is worth exploring the peninsula on which Nelson's Dockyard stands. At the southern tip is Snap-per Point, a barren area with cacti.

Indian Creek is another important site because archaeological excavations suggest it is the site of the first Amerindian settlement within the national park. Arawak and Carib relics have been unearthed.

This is a great area for exploring the rich marine life that teems in the inshore waters protected by the coral reef.

Shirley Heights

Shirley Heights is south of the Interpretation Centre and offers a delightful walk through the woods, and an insight into how strongly fortified the area was. The Heights are littered with the remains of the old gun emplacements, batteries, powder magazines and barracks of Fort Shirley. The area is named after General Sir Thomas Shirley, who was appointed Governor of the Leeward Islands in 1781 and served for ten years. He immediately set about building fortifications around the island, and the massive Fort Shirley took ten years to complete. There is a small museum in the area known as the Royal Artillery Quarters, which traces the history and development of the fort.

The Lookout Trail winds through the Shirley Heights Forest with its red-barked turpentine trees, cinnamon and loblolly trees. The leaves of the loblolly were used to make a tea which was given as a purgative, and this led nineteenth-century Royal Navy sailors to call any ship's medicine 'loblolly'. The Shirley Heights Lookout has been built, incorporating some of the old military remains, and offers wonderful views across English Harbour and the surrounding fortifications. It is easy to see how effective the cannon would have been in protecting the seaward approaches from attack.

A late afternoon tradition every Sunday, and now on Thursday as well, is for tourists and locals alike to gather to watch the fabulous sunset to the sounds of a steel band, and then enjoy a barbecue and drinks including local rum. An intriguing mix of old and new greets you as you look out over the old naval dockyard with its centuries-old traditions, while listening to the pulsating rhythms of the drummers and the latest reggae hits. You can also get to Shirley Heights along Fig Tree Drive.

The Friends of English Harbour are now preserving the area around Charlotte Peninsula, the site of the Carpenter family home dating back to 1750. The huge sandstone pillars rising from the sea below Shirley Heights are known locally as the Pillars of Hercules.

Mamora Bay is popular with scuba divers and snorkellers because of the Mamora Reef which is noted for its beautiful corals.

Back to St John's

Follow the coast road round Willoughby Bay through Christian Hill to Bethesda, and then round the head of the bay to Fort William, with the Horse Shoe Reef offshore.

Half Moon Bay is considered by many to be the island's most beautiful beach, but there are many other rivals. The shape of the bay and its exposure to the Atlantic means that it can be affected by a wide range of different conditions along the beach, with some areas experiencing only a gentle swell while others have crashing surf. There is a stables close to the beach if you fancy a horse ride through the surf. Also nearby is the Half Moon Bay Hotel and golf course.

Exchange Bay is the home of the Mill Reef Club.

You have to retrace your route, then head north through Freetown, so named because it was founded by freed slaves after Emancipation in 1834, to **Harmony Hall**, which looks out over Nonsuch Bay. The Hall, originally the Great House of Brown's Bay Mill, is built round an old sugar mill. The mill now houses a round bar and has an observation deck that offers fabulous

Fort James

The fort was built on the headland overlooking St John's, between 1704 and 1706, on the site of a 1670s fortification. It was named in 1734 after King James II and its purpose was to protect St John's Harbour and the sea approaches from attacks by pirates, especially french corsairs, from nearby Guadeloupe to the south.

Extended in the 1740s and again in 1773, its massive walls that have survived the centuries date from about 1740. The fort's weaponry was increased to 36 cannon during the American Revolution, and although never fired in anger, one was fired each day at sun-up and sundown, and whenever a visiting warship arrived.

Today there are 10 or so of these huge cannon, each weighing more than 2 tons (2,000kg), to add to the atmosphere and your photographs. Each massive cannon needed a gun crew of 12 men. The fort is worth visiting both for the history and for the tremendous views.

A visit to the laid-back Caribbean islands of Antigua and Barbuda doesn't mean cutting back on luxury. Antigua and Barbuda's accommodation ranges from luxury all-inclusive resorts and spacious villas to historic inns and intimate beachfront apartments. (Photo Credit: Mark L. Craighead)

views. There is also a good restaurant and a beach nearby where you can have a swim. More importantly, Harmony Hall features the work of local artists and craftsmen in an art gallery and studios, and stages an annual craft fair. It is open daily from l0am to 6pm ☎ 460-4120.

Again, retrace your route to the main road, turn right, then left at the T-junction. Pass the service station on your left and skirt the Potworks Dam Reservoir to the north, and then take the secondary road on your left through Freemans, heading west to connect with the main road back to St John's.

Tour 2 – The North

Drive north out of St John's, turn left at the Barrymore Hotel and then keep on the roads which follow the sea. The road runs out at Fort James.

This stretch of coastline north of St John's is the most heavily developed on the island, with many hotels looking out over Runaway Bay and Dickenson Bay where there are the remains of another of the island's defensive network of eighteenth-century forts. This is also a

Intimate beachfront apartment. (Photo Credit: Antigua and Barbuda Ministry of Tourism)

popular area for wealthy Antiguans to build their large, luxury homes.

The coast runs north past Weatherills Point and Soldier Point to Boon Point, the northernmost tip of the island. Follow the coast road round through Cedar Grove to Hodges Bay, which has a number of resort hotels, and also boasts the island's oldest house although it is not open to the public. It is an old Great House dating from the early seventeenth century. The road continues to Beggars Point, another area with hotels and restaurants and the Gambles Golf Course. On Sandy Lane, behind the Hodges Bay Club, is Aiton Place, the home and studio of artist and film-maker Nick Maley. He also has a gallery on Heritage Quay.

The road then runs south along the coast past Shoal Point and the island's

St Peter's Anglican Church

The unusual octagonal Italianate church in Parham was designed by Thomas Weekes and built in the 1840s to replace the original 1711 wooden church which burned down, and the 1754 replacement which was dismantled to make way for the new building. It has recently been restored and is noted for its ribbed wooden ceiling and the craftsmanship of the masonry. It has been described as the finest church in the British West Indies and it still has some of the original stucco work.

Betty's Hope

Journey back in time to Antigua's first large-scale sugar estate. Betty's Hope was established in 1650 by Governor Christopher Keynell. The owners fled when the French occupied the island for 6 months in 1666, and in 1674 the estate was taken over by Sir Christopher Codrington, who named it after his daughter. It remained in the Codrington family for almost 300 years. In effect, Betty's Hope was the seat of government for the whole of the Leeward Islands as successive members of the Codrington family served as Governor-General from the late 17th century until some way into the 18th century.

Sugar Mill – Betty's Hope, which was built in 1674, is the site of one of the first full-scale sugar plantations on Antigua, and offers a chance to step back into time by visiting the restored mills. (Photo Credit: Antigua and Barbuda Ministry of Tourism)

There are many old ruins and remains, and of special interest are the twin towers of the wind-driven sugar mills, and the arches that supported the boiling house. The sugar mill is the only working, authentic windmill in the Caribbean and the crushing mill was supplied in the mid-19th-century by Fletchers of Derby, England.

The original machinery had all been removed after the mill fell into disrepair, and the restoration team had to scour Antigua and surrounding islands for replacement parts and then had to figure out how to reconstruct a 19th-century working mill.

The estate, now operated by Betty's Hope Trust, is open to the public from Tuesday to Saturday, and is well signposted.

defence regiment base to Barnacle Point, with Maiden Island offshore and low-lying Long Island just beyond. Long Island was once used for raising cattle, which explains why its northern promontory is called Pasture Point. Today it is the home of the Jumby Bay Resort, for those who really want to get away from it all. Guests land at the international airport and are then ferried across to their own tropical island.

The road then runs inland towards the VC Bird International Airport, but take the secondary road along the coast with Fitches Creek inland and Fitches Creek Bay on your left. Continue on the secondary road to Parham, one of the oldest settlements on the island but although many claim it used to be the capital, this is not the case.

There are still a number of old buildings and traditional clapboard houses nestling among the palms close to the water and a fort still stands guard over the town and waters beyond.

North of Parham Harbour is **Fitches Creek**, which has another charming little church. St George's Church was built in the late 1680s, although extensively rebuilt in the 1730s and again at the beginning of the twentieth century. It contains the marble scroll from the grave of the first English settler to be buried in a place of worship on the island in 1659. Part of its charm lies in its setting, which looks out over spectacular seascapes.

You can explore Crabs Peninsula with Guiana Island just offshore. Then return to Parham and head south on the main road, turning left for Pares

and continuing east through Glanvilles and Willikies to visit **Indian Town National Park**. The park lies on a narrow peninsula that juts out into the sea and takes the full force of the Atlantic rollers which crash in. These waves have carved out the Devil's Bridge, a natural arch formed by the erosion of the soft limestone.

There are also several blowholes in the surrounding rocks. Blowholes are usually formed as a result of the continuous action of the water carving out a tunnel or cave in a stratum of soft rock. When the end of the tunnel collapses water shoots along it and then explodes out and upwards through the blowhole. The intensity of the blowout obviously depends on the strength of the surf. It's great fun trying to click the camera just at the right moment to capture the event on film.

Arawak relics have been found in this area, so there may have been early settlements here.

Retrace your route towards Pares but turn off left and follow the signs to Betty's Hope (see box opposite).

Back to St John's

Head back to the main road, turn left and continue through Pares to the T-junction. Turn right and then left again at Vernons, for the road back into St John's through Potters Village and St Johnston Village.

You can take a small detour south on the road opposite the abandoned sugar factory to **Sea View Farm**, a traditional pottery village where pots are still made from local clay.

BARBUDA

Barbuda lies less than 30 miles (49km) north of Antigua and offers some of the finest, longest natural beaches in the Caribbean, while the heavily wooded hinterland – with the Highlands in the north rising to 130 feet (40m) above the sea – is a naturalist's paradise. Barbuda also boasts the best-tasting lobster in the Caribbean.

Reefs lie off the north, east and south-east coasts, and there are exten-

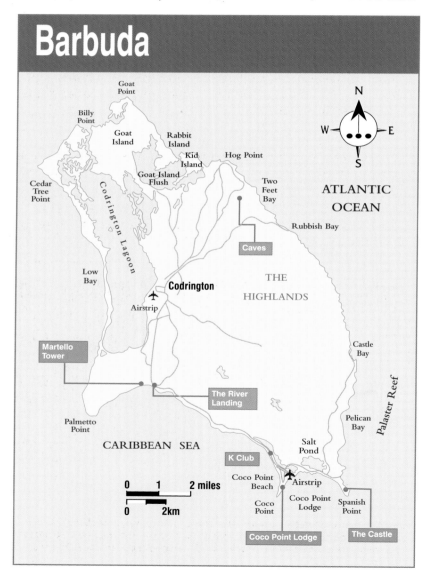

Getting Around

By Air

Barbuda is only a 15-minute hop from Antigua and makes a great day out if you can't stay for longer. Carib Aviation flies from Antigua daily at 8am and 6pm, while flights from Barbuda leave at 8.30am and 6.30pm.

Carib Aviation also flies charter to Barbuda, tailored to suit your special needs.

By Sea

Boats can be chartered for the four-hour crossing from Antigua, and a number of companies offer boats, either crewed or bare-board (see yachting section in FactFile).

By Car

The best way to get around is by car, although there are only a handful available for rent. Passing cars stop to give you a lift but the roads are not exactly busy.

Other ways to see the island are by foot, or taking a boat to reach secluded beaches, the bird reserve and so on.

Can You Keep a Secret? – Antigua's sister island, Barbuda, is perhaps one of the best kept secrets of the Caribbean, with miles and miles of untouched, pristine white and pink sand beaches. (Photo Credit: Antigua and Barbuda Ministry of Tourism)

The Codrington Lease

Poor soil excluded Barbuda from intensive sugar cane cultivation and consequently the island was used largely for rearing livestock. This accounts for many of the place names, such as Goat Island, Goat Point, Billy Point, Rabbit Island, Hog Point and so on. In 1685 King Charles II granted the Codrington family a fifty-year lease in return for a peppercorn rent of 'one fat sheep'. The family retained the lease until 1870, even though the island had been officially ceded to Antigua ten years earlier. Apart from the land, the family had rights to 'all wreckage' and as there were many shipwrecks on the offshore reefs, this boosted their fortunes considerably. There are still lots of goats. Agriculture and fishing are the main industries.

sive marshes in the southern part of the inland. The Highlands contain many caves, most of which have not been thoroughly explored.

In the old days the islanders supplemented their income as wreckers. Lights would be erected on a promontory so that passing ships would be tricked into thinking they were close to a settlement. The ships would head for the coast and founder on the reefs, where their freight would be salvaged by the waiting islanders.

Most of the island's population lives in the main settlement of **Codrington Village**, a collection of clapboard houses and a handful of streets.

The village is on Codrington Lagoon, the largest lagoon in the Caribbean, which teems with fish and the famous Barbuda lobsters.

The main airstrip is just to the south of Codrington Village. There is a second airstrip servicing the exclusive Coco Point Lodge in the south-east corner of the island in its own secluded 164 acres (66 hectares). The 1,200 islanders

rely heavily on the sea for their living, and it is said that there are more turtles on the island than locals.

Visitors love Barbuda for its very laid-back atmosphere, the stunning beaches and world-class diving and snorkelling. The longest stretch of beach extends for 7 miles (11km) and at certain times of the year the sand takes on a pink hue, the result of millions of tiny pieces of crushed coral and shell being washed ashore.

Over the last three centuries many ships have foundered on the offshore reefs which enclose the island, and the 73 charted sites offer excellent dives. Scuba equipment is not available on Barbuda outside the two resorts, although Antiguan dive operators run trips to the island.

The beaches around the island are also great for beachcombing; you never know what may be washed up from one of the wreck sites!

For naturalists there are the Highland woods which are home to wild pigs and fallow deer, introduced by the Codrington family and allowed to roam free.

The lagoons and mangrove swamps, as well as the bird sanctuary on the north-west coast, are the places for birdwatchers.

A limited number of seasonal deer hunting licences are available from the police station in Codrington Village. Other game includes blue wing teal, white cheeks, pigeons and guinea fowl.

Places to visit

There are several caves in the northern Highlands part of the island, most of which remain unexplored, although several of those that have bear petroglyphs carved by Arawaks. **Dark Cave**, inland from Two Feet Bay, is at least 300 feet (91m) deep, while inland between Pigeon Cliff and Castle Bay is the **Darby Sink Cave** – 300 feet (91m) across and 80 feet (24m) deep.

Highland House, situated at 124 feet (38m), the highest point on the island, was built by the Codrington family in 1750 as their official home on the island, but it was seldom used as they preferred to stay on Antigua. It has long since fallen into ruins, with only a few walls and some shells of outbuildings remaining, mostly covered by vines and other vegetation.

The **River Fort Martello Tower** is on the south coast and was built to protect the island's original quay. The 56-foot-high (17m) tower remains, although the nine cannon which were mounted on the gun emplacement on top have long since gone.

Palaster Reef off the south-east coast is a National Marine Park containing the wrecks of at least 60 ships. The most southerly part of the island is Spanish Point with the remains of the **Spanish Point Tower**, often called the Castle.

Nearby, Amerindian sites have been found dating back 2,000 years. There are two exclusive resorts – the K Club and Coco Point Lodge - although more modest accommodation is also available.

REDONDA

This uninhabited rock is one of the strangest and smallest 'kingdoms' in the world. In 1865 an Irishman, Matthew Shiell, who lived on Montserrat, and happened to be sailing past, 'claimed' the tiny island for his son Philippe, who passed it on to the poet John Gawsworth. He declared himself King Juan I, and dispensed aristocratic titles on his literary friends, including J.B. Priestley, Dylan Thomas and Rebecca West.

People did live on the island in the second half of the nineteenth century, mining the guano – bird droppings that had accumulated over thousands of years from the huge colonies of nesting birds. The guano was shipped out as a plant food.

There was once a tiny post office on the island and Redonda stamps are rare and highly collectible.

The current 'king' resides in Sussex, and his thousands of 'subjects' are made up of seabirds, lizards and a few goats. The only way to see Redonda is to charter a boat to take you there.

The pristine and relatively untouched islands of Antigua and Barbuda make for the perfect "unplugged" getaway. (Photo Credit: Antigua and Barbuda Ministry of Tourism)

The Magnificent Frigate Bird

The Barbuda bird sanctuary, on an area of Codrington Lagoon overgrown with squat mangroves, is home to the magnificent frigate bird, and is best reached by launch. It is the largest colony of these birds in the Lesser Antilles. The birds, which have a wingspan of up to 90 inches (2.3m), are often called man o' war birds, because they are, in every sense, hunters of the ocean. The birds catch fish close to the surface but, remarkably for birds that spend most of their lives over the water, their feathers are not waterproof; if their plumage gets wet they cannot fly. Because of this, the birds cannot dive into the water to catch fish, so they have to become pirates, swooping on other birds to make them drop their catches which are often caught in mid-air. On Barbuda the birds are not disturbed by humans and are almost tame.

The frigate bird can be spotted by its long forked tail, pointed wings, streamlined silhouette and vicious curved bill. It soars effortlessly on the wind and its habit of opening and closing its tail feathers for direction gives it the Caribbean patois name of 'siso' (scissors). The adult male is black and has a scarlet throat pouch which is inflated like a balloon during courtship rituals, while the female has a white breast and sides. The young of both sexes have white heads and breasts. A single egg is laid in a crude nest of sticks and the young bird is dependent on its mother for at least a year.

The unspoiled island of Barbuda is home to the only Frigate Bird Sanctuary in the Caribbean, providing a unique experience for nature-lovers and ornithologists. (Photo Credit: Antigua and Barbuda Ministry of Tourism)

A beach of a different colour – Barbuda, a low-lying coral island, is known for its untouched pink coral sand beaches. (Photo Credit: Antigua and Barbuda Ministry of Tourism)

Bird Life

Today the island of Burbuda still attracts birdwatchers for its many different species of seabirds and particularly for the Burrowing Owl which is now extinct in Antigua. The owl is easily distinguishable from other owls because of its long legs, which give it added height when on the ground. It is nocturnal, nests in pairs or small colonies, and often perches in the entrance to its burrow during the day. It has developed a mechanism to defend itself when disturbed in its burrow – it imitates the sound of a rattlesnake.

On the unplugged island of Barbuda, it's hard to tell where the ocean meets the sky. (Photo Credit: Antigua and Barbuda Ministry of Tourism)

Eating Out

Note: Most restaurants, but not all, accept credit cards, so check first.
$ - Inexpensive
$$ - Average
$$$ - Expensive

Abracadabra

Nelson's Dockyard. English Harbour, Italian. Try the delicious home-made pasta and fresh lobster. There is a popular video bar with live reggae music on Tuesday, a band on Thursday, and a DJ every Friday and Saturday. Open nightly.
☎ 460-2701
$$

The Admiral's Inn

Nelson's Dockyard, West Indian and International. Dine in the historic Georgian Inn or outside under the trees with stunning views over English Harbour. Open daily for breakfast, lunch and dinner. Closed Sept. Reservations recommended.
☎ 460-1027
$$-$$$

Alberto's

Willoughby Bay, Italian. Open for dinner in the charming gazebo with seafood and Italian dishes, accompanied by great wines. You can even tour the wine cellar to select your own bottle. It is open nightly except Mon and closed over the summer. Reservations recommended.
☎ 460-3007
$$-$$$

Al Porto Ristorante & Bar

Jolly Harbour, Italian. A lively restaurant offering pizzas, pastas and seafood and open-air dining. The restaurant is open daily from 10am to late, and happy hour is from 6pm to 7pm each evening.
☎ 462-7695
$$-$$$

Al Solvefito

Hodges Bay, Italian.
☎ 462-5387

Aly's Roti and Grill Shop

20 Long Street, St John's, Caribbean.
☎ 460-7684
$

The Andes Restaurant & Bar

Royal Antiguan Resort, seafood and Caribbean. The restaurant overlooks Deep Bay and is named after a ship that sank there in 1907. Great seafood and steaks and nightly reggae, calypso and jazz groups. There is a Wed night barbecue and Friday night Caribbean buffet. It is open for lunch and dinner daily.
☎ 462-3733
$$$

Bay House

Tradewinds. One of Antigua's first eateries which showcases local dishes and local produce. Excellent wine list. Dinner served from 6pm to 10.30pm.
☎ 462-1223
$$$

Bayside

Sandals Grand Antigua. Seafood specialists in a friendly, intimate, waterfront atmosphere.
$$$

Blue Lagoon

Deep Bay, Five Islands, International/Seafood.
☎ 460-6060

The Beach

Dickenson Bay (formerly Spinnakers) offers classic dishes from around the world accompanied by excellent wines. Open for breakfast, lunch and dinner every day.
☎ 480-6940
$$–$$$

Big Banana

Jolly Harbour, Italian.
☎ 462-5387

Catherine's Cafe

Antigua Slipway, Island fare.
☎ 460-5050
$–$$

Chutney's

Fort Road, Indian
☎ 462-2977

Chez Pascal

Galley Bay, Gourmet French cuisine with fabulous views over the bay. The rack of lamb always gets rave reviews. Open for lunch and dinner from 11am to 11pm Tue to Sat.
☎ 462-3232
$$$

Colombo's

Galleon Beach Club, English Harbour, Italian. The restaurant is named after Columbus's landing place, so it is appropriate that there is an Italian restaurant on the site. Excellent authentic Italian cooking featuring home-made pastas, lobster and veal specials, with the added bonuses of wonderful scenery and a relaxed atmosphere. It is open daily for lunch and dinner.
☎ 460-1452
$$–$$$

Crazy Horse Saloon

Lower Redcliffe Quay, Bar & Grill.
☎ 462-7936

Curtain Bluff Restaurant

Curtain Bluff Hotel, Old Road, Morris Bay, International. Fine dining in a charming atmosphere and noted for both its seafood dishes and superb wine list. The wine cellar has 25,000 bottles. The restaurant is open daily for lunch and dinner Mon to Sat between mid-Oct and mid-May. Dinner reservations are necessary and men are expected to wear jacket and tie.
☎ 462-8400
$$$

Food Court at Woods Centre

Woods Centre, Antiguan, Chinese, Italian.

Eating Out

The Frenchman

Runaway Bay. Recently open and set in tropical gardens, chef Bruno offers classic French and Caribbean cuisine. Open for lunch 10am–5pm and dinner 6pm onwards.
☎ 562-1545
$$$

Harmony Hall

Freetown, seafood and Caribbean. The views over Nonsuch Bay from the round bar in the sugar mill are tremendous, as is the seafood offered at lunch and dinner. The lobster is wonderful. The restaurant is open daily from 10am to 6pm and snacks are served during the afternoon. Apart from the food, the place is worth visiting for the displays of Caribbean arts and crafts which can, of course, be purchased.
☎ 460-4120
$$–$$$

Golden Bowl

Church Street, Chinese.
☎ 462-4505

Home

Gambles Terrace. Excellent classic gourmet Caribbean cuisine using the finest, freshest local produce and herbs from the kitchen garden. Open for dinner from 6.30pm Mon to Sat.
☎ 461-7651
$$–$$$

Hawksbill Beach Resort

Five Islands. West Indian seafood and Continental, casually elegant dining inside or on the terrace.
☎ 462-0301
$$$

Hemingway's

St Mary's Street, St John's. West Indian and International. Dine out on the deck, which catches the gentle breeze, and enjoy great seafood and island dishes. It is open Mon to Sat from 8.30am.
☎ 462-2763
$$

The Hub

Soul Alley, St John's. Island fare, live jazz.
☎ 462-9442

The Inn at English Harbour

West Indian and International. A great place for a meal at any time of the day, but especially if you want a romantic dinner. Dining on the terrace by candlelight, with the yachts bobbing in the water and Nelson's Dockyard and Freeman's Bay as the backdrop, is a truly memorable occasion. The á la carte menu changes daily to ensure only the freshest of produce is served, and outstanding dishes include seafood, Thai curries and West Indian dishes. The restaurant is open daily but closed from early Sept to mid-Oct.
☎ 460-1014
$$–$$$

Joe Mike's

Joe Mike's Hotel Plaza, Caribbean.
☎ 462-1142

Julian's

Church Street & Corn Alley, fine dining.
☎ 462-4766

Last Lemming

Falmouth. Great views and great food at this popular watering hole. catch the sunset over dinner or enjoy the outstanding Sunday brunch.
☎ 460-6910
$$–$$$

Le Bistro

Hodges Bay, French and International. Fine dining for those who truly appreciate it. Wonderful seafood creations, memorable sauces and a bill to match, but worth every cent. Open for dinner Tuesday to Sunday.
☎ 462-3881
$$$

Le Cap Horn

English Harbour, French and Argentinian. Great beef, seafood and lobster and tempting desserts. Open daily from 6.30pm to 11pm.
☎ 460-1194
$$–$$$

O'Gradys Pub

Lower Nevis Street, pub fare, live music, live jazz.
☎ 462-5392

Palm Restaurant

Blue Waters. Eat in the garden or on the terrace and enjoy sea views and great food from the á la carte or fixed price menu. Live entertainment most nights. Reservations recommended.
☎ 462-0290
$$–$$$

Pavilion

Pavilion Drive, Coolidge. Great food offering a mix of European and French cuisine. Fabulous wine list. Jackets required for dinner, reservations recommended.
☎ 480-6800
$$$

Peters Jolly

Harbour. Great fish and seafood. No Telephone.

Shirley Heights Lookout

Shirley Heights, West Indian and seafood. Dine in style with magnificent views over Nelson's Dockyard. Steel band concert accompanies the Thursday 3.30pm to 8pm barbecue, and the Sunday barbecue features six hours of live entertainment from 3pm to 9pm.
☎ 460-1785
$$–$$$

Sticky Wicket

20 Pavilion Drive, Caribbean cuisine and cricket. Very lively place. Open 2 days a week for lunch and dinner.
☎ 481-7000
$$–$$$

Tamarind

Palm Bay Beach Club, Browns Bay, Italian and seafood specialties. The lobster and fish are delivered daily so couldn't be fresher. Open for lunch and dinner Tue to Sun.
☎ 460-4174
$$–$$$

Arrival, Entry Requirements and Customs

Visitors who are citizens of Canada and the United States, and are not planning to stay for more than six months, must have a valid passport. Visitors from Britain, the European Union, Australia and Japan require a valid passport while most other visitors require a visa, so check with your travel company. You may also be asked to show a return air ticket, and evidence of pre-arranged accommodation and adequate means of support. An immigration form has to be filled in and presented on arrival. The form requires you to say where you will be staying on the island, and if you plan to move around, put down the first hotel you will be staying at. The immigration form is in two parts, one of which is stamped and returned to you in your passport. You must retain this until departure, when the slip is retrieved as you check in at the airport.

If visiting on business, a letter confirming this may prove helpful in speeding your way through customs, especially if you are carrying samples.

Having cleared immigration you will have to go through customs, and it is quite usual to have to open your luggage for inspection. If you have expensive cameras, electrical goods, etc it is a good idea to travel with photocopies of the receipts.

When entering Antigua your duty-free allowance is 200 cigarettes, 50 cigars or 250g (9oz) of tobacco, 1 litre/liter of spirits or wine and 170ml (6oz) of perfume.

Accommodation

There is a wide range of accommodation to suit all tastes and pockets, from top class hotels to delightful guest houses, self-catering apartments, luxury villas and beach cottages. There are about 4,200 hotel rooms on Antigua and Barbuda, with a total of 6,500 beds. Almost all hotels and apartments are close to or on the beach, most rooms are air conditioned or have ceiling fans, and most properties offer a wide range of sports and entertainment.

If you want to eat out and explore quite a lot it pays to stay in a hotel offering board only. If you want to laze on the beach and not stray far from the hotel, choose a hotel package offering meals as well.

There are also apartments, holiday villas and beach cottages available for short and long rent, offering you the privacy of your own accommodation and the flexibility to eat in or out, with cooks and maid service available if required. The 'high season' runs from mid-December to mid-April and prices tend to be lower at other times. There are no youth hostel or camping facilities on the islands.The following is not meant to be a comprehensive list but all hotels mentioned have been visited by the author.

Some terms

AI - All inclusive

MAP - Modified American Plan (breakfast and dinner are included)

EP - European Plan (bed only and no meals)

AP - American Plan (room and all meals)

Prices quoted by hotels are for rooms, whether one or two people are sharing, and you may find it difficult to get a reduction if you are visiting alone, but have a go. $ represents inexpensive accommodation, $$ moderate, and $$$ deluxe.

Antigua

HOTELS

Admiral's Inn

English Harbour. A delightful, restored Georgian weathered brick building dating from 1788, with huge hand-hewn beams in the heart of Nelson's Dockyard National Park.

☎ 460-1153/1027

Fax 460-1534

$$ EP

Amarylis

Airport Road, comfortable 22-room hotel close to the airport, with Calypso Café.

☎ 462-8690

Fax 462-0375

$$

Antigua Village

Dickenson Bay, a delightful Mediterranean-style villa development 2 miles (3km) from St John's, and 5 miles (8km) from the airport. Set in lovely tropical gardens beside the sea, it offers 56 air-conditioned studios and one and two-bedroom apartments, all with kitchens plus two restaurants.

☎ 462-2930

Fax 462-0375

$$–$$$ EP

Barrymore Beach Club

Fort Road, is 2 miles (3km) from St John's and 7 miles (11km) from the airport, and set in tropical gardens alongside a fabulous white sand, palm-fringed beach.

☎ 462-1055 Fax 462-4140

$$–$$$ EP

Blue Waters

Set in magnificent tropical gardens on its own private bay with two white sand beaches. It has 77 rooms and suites and one-to-three bedroom beachside villas. Facilities include two restaurants – the open-air Palm Restaurant and the à la carte Vyvian's Restaurant – bars, beauty spa, watersports, snorkelling with nearby golf, casinos and discos

☎ 462-0290 Fax 462-0293

$$

Carlisle Bay Old Road

A new contemporary, luxury resort on the unspoilt south coast. It features 80 suites, hotel spa, pool, tennis, a variety of watersports and children's club. There are two restaurants and three bars plus a private cinema.

☎ 484-0000

$$$ EP

Catamaran Hotel and Marina

Falmouth Harbour, offers 16 waterside rooms close to Nelson's Dockyard. Facilities include restaurant and bar, sunfish, rowing boats, snorkelling and deep sea fishing.
☎ 460-1036
$ EP

Jolly Beach Resort

Set on a bluff between two beaches and overlooking Jolly Bay. There are six spacious gingerbread cottages, an award-winning restaurant, watersports, snorkeling, and nearby tennis, squash, golf, shopping and restaurants.
☎ 460-2626
Fax 462-9423
$$–$$$

Coco Bay Resort

Valley Church, new exclusive resort of four pastel-coloured cottages, restaurant, pool, sailing and watersports.
☎ 462-2400
Fax 462-2424
$$$

Copper and Lumber Store Hotel

English Harbour. The hotel offers 13 studios and suites in a lovely old building set in wel-tended gardens. There is a boat shuttle to nearby beaches. The Wardroom restaurant is noted for its cuisine, and there is a traditional English-style pub offering draught beers and bar snacks.
☎ 460-1058
Fax 460-1529
$$$ EP

Cortsland Hotel

Upper Gables, a delightful country inn set in tropical gardens and close to the airport and St John's.
☎ 462-1395 Fax 462-1699
$ EP

Curtain Bluff Resort

Old Road. This modern all-inclusive resort sits in lush tropical gardens at the end of the private Curtain Bluff peninsula which runs between two beautiful beaches.
☎ 462-8400
Fax 462-8409
$$$ AI

Dian Bay Resort

Dian Bay. An intimate, secluded resort set in tropical gardens with 50 de-luxe rooms 2 three-tiered, swimming pool and full service spa. Currently closed until winter season 2009.
☎ 460-6646
$$$

Dickenson Bay Cottages

Offers one, two and three-bedroom cottages on the hillside over looking the bay and set in beautiful tropical gardens.
☎ 462-4940
Fax 462-4941
$$

Dove Cove

Close to St John's, 12 all-suite apartments set in tropical gardens with pool.
☎ 463-8600 Fax 463-8601
$$

Falmouth Beach Apartments,

Falmouth Harbour. There are 20 fully equipped, self-catering studio apartments either on or close to the beach.
☎ 460-1027 Fax 460-1534
$$ EP

Galley Bay Resort

Galley Bay, Beach Road. An all-inclusive resort with 90 luxury rooms and suites set in 40 acres of tropical grounds and next to a bird sanctuary. There is reef snorkelling just yards from the beach.

☎ 462-0302
$$$ AI

Galleon Beach Club

Freemans Bay, beachside villas, restaurant, tennis, sailing, watersports.

☎ 460-1024
Fax 460-1450
$$-$$$

Harmony Hall

Brown's Bay. There are six spacious rooms in two villas providing B&B accommodation.

☎ 460-4120
$$

Hawksbill Beach Resort

Five Islands. Set in 37 acres (15 hectares) of lovely tropical gardens overlooking the sweeping bay and four exclusive beaches with restaurant, tennis, pool and watersports – one clothing optional.

☎ 462-0301
Fax 462-1515
$$$ EP

Heritage Hotel

Heritage Quay, St Mary's Street, St John's. Studio and one and two-bedroom suites, ideal for business visitors. Facilities include meeting rooms, secretarial services with all amenities close by.

☎ 462-1247
Fax 462-1179
$-$$ EP

Hodges Bay Club Resort

Hodges Bay, offers comfort, luxury and privacy. All villas have private balconies with sea views, and facilities include restaurant, bar, swimming pool, children's wading-pool, tennis and watersports.

☎ 462-2300
Fax 462-1962
$$-$$$ EP

The Inn at English Harbour

There are 6 hillside rooms and 22 beachfront rooms in the two-storey property in a corner of Freeman's Bay on ten acres (4 hectares) of national park beside the white sand beach and set among the palm trees.

☎ 460-1014 Fax 460-1603
$$$ EP

Jolly Beach Resort

Lignumvitae Bay, 12 miles (19km) from the airport and 7 miles (11km) from St John's. The all-inclusive resort has 464 rooms and 6 villas set in 40 acres (16 hectares) of tropical gardens on the one-mile (1.6km) long Jolly Beach. It offers 4 restaurants and 6 bars, mini casino, pool, floodlit tennis, children's club, disco, live entertainment nightly, daily activities, free bikes, scuba sailing and watersports. There are also wedding and honeymoon packages.

☎ 462-0061 (UK 01372-466944,
US 1-800-777-1250)
Fax 462-4900
$$$

Jolly Harbour Beach Resort

Offers 20 self-contained privately-owned beachfront villas, some with their own moorings.

☎ 462-6166 Fax 462-6167
$$

Jolly Harbour Marina Sports Centre and Golf Club

Lignumvitae Bay. Situated on a magnificent beach and in a complex covering 500 acres (200 hectares).
☎ 462-3085
Fax 462-7686
$$ EP

Jumbo Bay

Long Island, 300-acre (120 hectare) resort with 68 rooms and 12 villas, pool, spa, tennis. ☎ 421-9016
$$$

Mango Bay Hotel and Beach Club

A 64 room all-inclusive resort overlooking Dian Bay on the north-east corner of the island. There is a thatched lagoon-side restaurant, three-tier swimming pool and private beach.
☎ 463-2003
Fax 463-2425
$$$ AI

Marina Bay Beach Resort

Dickenson Bay, 27 beachside suites.
☎ 462-3254
Fax 462-2151
$$

Pelican Isle Villas

Johnsons Point, Turners Beach, 7 villas overlooking the beach with fishing, boating and diving.
☎ 462-8385
Fax 462-4361
$$–$$$

Rex Bhie Heron Beach Hotel

Johnson's Point. This two-floor 64-room beachside property enjoys a sheltered position because of the hills behind. The hotel has a terrace restaurant and bar, live entertainment most nights, and offers windsurfing, sailing, scuba, snorkelling, waterskiing and beautiful beaches.
☎ 462-8567
Fax 462-8005
$$ EP

Rex Halcyon Cove Beach Resort

Dickenson Bay. There are 226 luxury, spacious rooms and suites set in beautiful tropical flower gardens running down to the white sand beach and turquoise water. Facilities include tennis with floodlit courts, freshwater swimming pool, free sailing, windsurfing, pedalos, snorkelling, water-skiing, scuba and deep sea fishing. There are also shops, boutiques, live entertainment, 2 restaurants – Warri Pier and The Terrace – and 4 bars.
☎ 460-0256
Fax 462-0271
$$$ EP/MAP

Royal Antiguan Beach and Tennis Resort

Deep Bay. A luxury high-rise resort with 282 rooms and 12 one-bedroom garden and poolside cottages scattered through the extensive 150 acres (60 hectares) of lush, tropical gardens alongside a half-mile (800m) long beach. Facilities include 3 restaurants, 5 bars, casino, boutiques, gym, hair salon, floodlit tennis, tennis pro shop, scuba and dive shop, pool, windsurfing, water-skiing, kayaks, sailing, entertainment, children's playground and shopping arcade. It has extensive conference and banqueting facilities and also offers honeymoon packages.
☎ 462-3733
Fax 462-3732
$$$ EP

Runaway Beach Club

Runaway Bay, 24 beachfront rooms, restaurant.

☎ 462-1318

$$

St James's Club

Mamora Bay. Occupies 100 acres (40 hectares) of a private peninsula jutting out into the mouth of the bay. There are 72 two-bedroom villas, 164 suites and rooms with bay or ocean view.

☎ 460-5000

Fax 460-3015

$$$ EP

Sandals Grande Antigua Resort & Spa

Dickenson Bay. A luxury all-inclusive couples-only resort set in 19 acres (7.6 hectares) of tropical, manicured gardens. It has 149 luxuriously decorated rooms, a choice of 3 restaurants and bars, live entertainment, disco, 5 swimming pools, jacuzzis, health spa, floodlit tennis, watersports and planned activities.

☎ 462-0267

Fax 462-4135

$$$ AI

Sandpiper Reef Resort

A new 22-room and 2-suite resort 10 minutes from the airport and close to the Cedar Valley Golf Course.

☎ 462-0939 Fax 462-1743

$$

Sibenay Beach Club

Dickenson Bay, an en-suite hotel, set in beachside tropical gardens with pool, watersports and award-winning restaurant.

☎ 462-0806 Fax 462-3356

$$$

Sunsail Club Colonna

Close to the airport this 100-room apartment and villa property boasts the biggest pool on the island. There are two restaurants: a buffet-style beach restaurant and The Coast – offering seafood and international dishes. There are three bars including the Sugar Mill Bar which provides gentle late night music and an American games room.

☎ 462-6263

Fax 462-6430

$–$$

Sunset Cove

Runaway Bay, 33 self-contained suites, with restaurant, bar and nightclub, beauty salon, shops and watersports.

☎ 462-3762

Fax 462-2684

$$

Trafalgar Beach Villas

Pillar Rock Bay. Set in 5 acres (2 hectares) of gardens that run down to the secluded white sand beach.

☎ 462-2531

Fax 462-2548

$$–$$$ EP

Yepton Beach Resort

38 beachfront units set in 37 acres of landscaped gardens, with pool, tennis, croquet, watersports and restaurant.

$$–$$$

Real estate, property management and rental services

Caribbean Properties
PO Box 1559, Falmouth, Antigua.
☎ 462-1873

Tradewind Realty
Falmouth, Antigua
☎ 460-1082

Barbuda

Hotels

Accommodation on the island is limited and in demand, so early reservations are strongly recommended.

The Beach House

An exclusive resort with 21 rooms and suites for those who want the ultimate in pampering. Each guest is assigned their own 'Service Ambassador' to make sure they lack for nothing.
☎ 631-537-1352
$$$

The Coco Point Lodge

A discreet, exclusive, award-winning all-inclusive 34-room property on the beach which attracts the rich, the famous and the discerning, many of whom return year after year. It is set on a secluded 164-acre (66-hectare) peninsula close to the south-east tip of the island, and has been voted 'one of the most captivating resorts in the world' and described as 'simplicity with perfection'.

All the rooms, catering for a maximum of 68 guests, are in beachside bungalows and cottages, each with its own deck looking out over the Caribbean. The property, founded in 1960 by American entrepreneur William Cody Kelly and still owned by the Kelly family, is edged by 2.5 miles (4km) of white sand beach and surrounded by superb pristine beaches. It has its own lighted airstrip where guests arrive by private plane from Antigua's international airport. The resort is noted for its low-key luxury and comfort, qualities which bring back many of its guests year after year for the house party atmosphere created by Britons Caroline and Martin Price, who have been resident managers since 1980. The tropical garden restaurant serves the finest local lobster, seafood and freshly baked bread and pastries, and is noted for its home-made soups and bisques. It also imports the best produce from around the world including French cheeses and fine wines.

The all-inclusive facilities include all-weather tennis, sunfish, sailing, windsurfing, waterskiing, sea-kayaking, snorkelling and equipment, deep sea fishing aboard the 43-foot (13m) motor yacht *Barbuda Belle*, reef and bone fishing with tackle provided, and informal trap shooting. Vehicles are also available with local guides for sightseeing.
☎ 462-3816 Fax 462-5340 (US ☎ 212-986-1416)
$$$

Hotel Palmetto Resort

24 suites on a 35-mile (60km) stretch of white sand.

☎ 460-0442

Fax 460-0440

$$$

The K Club

The island's other exclusive, all-inclusive resort, owned by the world-famous Milanese designer Krizia. It has 42 beautiful rooms set in 230 acres (92 hectares) of tropical gardens alongside a 3.5-mile (5.6km) white sand beach. 35 of the rooms are villas and cottages with mini-kitchens and private balconies. Guests include the rich and famous, and are met on arrival in Antigua and flown to Barbuda in the Club's private 8-seater plane. The property has a 9-hole golf course, the only one on Barbuda. Facilities also include tennis, snorkelling, windsurfing, sunfish and sailboats. Fishing and scuba diving trips can be arranged.

☎ 460-0300

Fax 460-0305

$$$

Airlines/Airports

Air Canada
☎ 462-1147/800-422-6232

Air France
☎ 01159-082-6221

Air St Kitts-Nevis
☎ 465-8571

American Airlines
☎ 462-0950/800-433-7300

British Airways
☎ 462-0879/800-247-9297

Caribbean Airlines (formerly BWIA)
☎ 800-774-2225

Carib Aviation
☎ 462-3147

Caribbean Helicopters
☎ 460-5900

Condor/Lufthansa
☎ 462-0987/800-645-3880

Continental
☎ 462-5353/800-231-0856

Delta
☎ 800-532-4777

LIAT
☎ 480-5600/5700

Virgin
☎ 01293 747747

Banks

Most banks are open Monday to Thursday from 8am to 1pm and 3pm to 5pm, Friday from 8am to noon and 3pm to 5pm. Some bank branches also open on Saturday morning from 8am to noon or 1pm.

Antigua Barbuda Investment Bank
High Street and Corn Alley, St John's
☎ 480-2701

Antigua Commercial Bank
St Mary's and Thames Street, St John's
☎ 462-1217

Bank of Antigua
High and Thames Streets, St John's
☎ 480-2700

Nelson's Dockyard
☎ 460-1367

Airport Boulevard
☎ 480-5300

Bank of Nova Scotia
High Street, St John's
☎ 480-1500

Barclays Bank
High and Market Streets, St John's
☎ 480-5000

Caribbean Banking Corporation
High Street, St John's
☎ 462-4217

Royal Bank of Canada
High and Market Streets, St John's
☎ 480-1150

Swiss American Bank
Woods Estate, St John's
☎ 480-2246

Swiss-American National Bank of Antigua
High Street, St John's
☎ 480-2230
Branches at Heritage Quay, Friar's Hill Road, Nelson's Dockyard and Jolly Harbour.

Beaches/swimming

There are fabulous beaches, everything you ever dreamed of for a tropical island, long stretches of sand, a fringe of tall palms for shade, and turquoise, calm, clear warm seas. The beaches are clean, litter-free and seldom crowded. The eastern beaches facing the Atlantic tend to have larger surf, while the western beaches offer more sheltered swimming.

Antigua boasts 365 white sand beaches – one for every day of the year–and Barbuda has miles of beautiful beaches. The longest beach runs for 7 miles (11km) and at certain times the sand turns pink because of millions of tiny particles of crushed coral and shell that are washed ashore.

All the beaches on the islands are public. The only officially designated nude beach is a remote area on Five Islands beyond the Hawksbill Beach Resort.

Best beaches on Antigua include:

Carlisle Bay	Fort James Bay	Lignumvitae Bay
Darkwood	Galley Bay	Long Bay
Deep Bay	Half Moon Bay	Mamora Bay
Dickenson Bay	Hawksbill Bay	Rendezvous Bay
Doigs Beach	Johnsons Bay	Runaway Bay
Ffryes Bay	Jolly Beach	

Camping

There are no official campsites on the islands.

Car Rental/Driving

Cars, jeeps and other four-wheel-drive vehicles can be rented and provide the best way of exploring the islands. If you plan to go at peak periods it is best to rent your vehicle in advance through your travel agent. Cars can be rented, however, at airports, hotels or car rental offices on the island.

Car rental rates vary enormously but start from around US$40–50 a day for compact automatics, and from $50–60 for jeeps or other four-wheel-drive vehicles during the summer low season. Winter rates are usually a little more expensive. There is quite a wide range of vehicles available and rates depend both on the type of vehicle and the rental company. There are usually quite a lot of incentives, so it pays to shop around.

To rent a car you must have a valid driving licence which entitles you to receive a temporary 90-day local driving permit for a fee of EC$50 (US$20). You can get this at the airport or any police station, although most car rental companies now do this for you. An imprint of your credit card, which acts as a deposit, is usually required.

Before accepting the vehicle check it for scratches, dents and other problems, such as missing wing mirrors, and make sure these are clearly listed. Also check there is a spare wheel in good condition and a working jack. While there are several service stations around the island it is a good idea always to keep your fuel tank topped up.

DRIVE ON THE LEFT, stick to the speed limits and use a good map.

Driving under the influence of alcohol or drugs is against the law, and there are heavy penalties if convicted, especially as a result of an accident.

Avoid clearly marked 'no parking' zones or you might pick up a ticket, but parking generally does not pose a problem.

If you have an accident or breakdown during the day you should call your car rental company, so make sure you have the telephone number with you. They will usually send out a mechanic or a replacement vehicle. If you are stuck at night make sure the car is off the road, lock the vehicle and call a taxi to take you back to your hotel. Report the problem to the car rental company or the police as soon as possible.

Car and Scooter Rental companies

Archibald Rent A Car
Powells Estate
☎ 561-1709

Avis Rent A Car
VC Bird International Airport
☎ 462-AVIS/2840
St James's Club
☎ 462-5000

Bike Plus
Camacho's Avenue
☎462-2453

Dion's Auto Rentals Ltd
VC Bird International Airport
☎ 462-3466

Dollar Rent A Car
St John's and airport
☎ 462-0362

Hyatt Rent A Car
☎ 463-2012

Hertz Rent A Car
Airport Road
☎ 462-4114
Jolly Harbour
☎ 481-4456
VC Bird International Airport
☎ 481-4455

Holiday Car Rentals
Dickenson Bay
☎ 462-9780

Jacobs Car Rental
All Saints Road, St John's
☎ 462-0576

Jonas Rent A Car
Free pick-up from the airport and hotels
☎ 462-3760

Lion Car Rental
Airport Road
☎ 562-2708
English Harbour
☎ 463-7100

Oakland Rent A Car
VC Bird International Airport
☎ 462-3021

Payne Car Rental
VC Bird International Airport or free delivery and pick-up anywhere on the island
☎ 462-3009/460-9177/9988

Slane's Car Rental
Newgate Street
☎ 462-8789

Titi Rent A Car
Galleon Beach
☎ 460-1452

Thrifty Rent A Car
VC Bird International Airport and island-wide delivery service
☎ 462-9523/8803

Tropical Rentals
Valley Church Road
☎ 562-5180

JT's Rent A Scoot
Parham
☎ 463-3578

Paradise Boat Sales (Scooter Rentals)
Jolly Harbour
☎ 460-7125

Speedy Joe's
Nevis Street, St John's
☎ 462-1141

Casinos

King's Casino
Heritage Quay, St John's
☎ 462-1727

Royal Casino
Royal Antiguan Hotel
☎ 462-3733

St James Club
☎ 460-5000

Castle Harbour Club Casino
St John's

Casino Riveria
Runaway Bay, St James Club
☎ 460- 5000

Coral Reef Casino
Jolly Harbour
☎ 462-7775

Dickenson Cove Resort and Casino
☎ 462-0256

Flamingo Antiguan
Dickenson Bay
☎ 462-1266

Joe Mike's Downtown Hotel Plaza
St John's
☎ 462-9877

Pineapple Beach Club Casino
☎ 463-2006

Keno Palaca Casino
St Mary's Street, St John's
☎ 462-9877

Royal Antiguan Casino
☎ 462-3733

Churches

There are more than 100 churches on the island. Most of the people are Protestant, although many other faiths are represented, including Baha'i, Baptist, Church of Christ, Church of God, Jehovah's Witness, Methodist, Moravian, Pentecostal, Rastafarian, Roman Catholic and Seventh-Day Adventists.

Clothing

Casual is the keyword but you can generally be as smart or as cool as you like. There are a number of upmarket restaurants and clubs where there are dress codes, and if you plan to visit these, you should pack accordingly. Beachwear is fine for the beach and pool areas, but cover up a little for the street. Informal is the order of the day and night, and this is not the place for suits and ties or evening gowns, unless you really like dressing up for dinner. During the day, light, cotton, casual clothes are ideal for exploring in. During the evening a light jumper or wrap may sometimes be needed. It is fun to change for dinner but for men this normally means smart slacks or trousers, and for women a summer dress or similar. There are establishments, however, where sports coats or jackets are not out of place, and women can be as elegant as they wish.

If you plan to explore on foot, stout footwear and a good waterproof jacket are essential. Also, wear sunglasses and a hat to protect you from the sun during the hottest part of the day, and you will need sandals on the beach as the sand can get too hot to walk on in bare feet.

Currency

The official currency on the islands is the East Caribbean dollar (EC$), which is fixed to the US dollar at about EC$2.65 to US$1.The EC$ rate against sterling fluctuates, but a general rule of thumb is to work on EC$4=£1. US dollars are widely accepted, as are all major credit cards. Currency can be exchanged at banks at fixed exchange rates, and at many hotels and stores, although the rate may not be as advantageous.

The American Express Card is the official card of the island, and their representative is Antours, Long and Thames Streets, St John's ☎ 462-4788.

Note: Always have a few small denomination notes for tips.

Departure Tax

There is a EC$50/US$20 departure tax payable at the airport check-in.

Disabled Facilities

Many of the watersports and dive operations will accommodate disabled visitors. There are some facilities for the disabled at most of the larger resorts.

Drugs

There are strict laws prohibiting the possession and use of drugs, including marijuana. Heavy fines and prison await those who ignore the law.

Electricity

The usual electricity supply is either 110 volts or 220 AC, 60 cycles, the former being the more common and suitable for US appliances. Most hotels have dual voltages. Adapters are necessary for European appliances without dual voltages, and may be available from your hotel.

Embassies and Consulates

British High Commission, Old Parham Road, St John's	☎ 462-0008
Chinese Embassy, Mount Pleasant, Antigua	☎ 462-1125
Danish Consulate, High Street, St John's	☎ 480-3070
Dutch Consulate, High Street, St John's	☎ 481-1850
German Consulate, Hodges Bay, St John's	☎ 462-2824
Italian Consulate, Falmouth Harbour, Antigua	☎ 460-1543
Norwegian Consulate, High Street, St John's	☎ 462-0858
US Consular Office, Falmouth, Antigua	☎ 463-5631
Venezuelan Embassy, Friar's Hill Road, Antigua	☎ 462-1574

Essential Things to Pack

Sun block cream, sunglasses, sun hat, camera, insect repellent, binoculars if interested in birdwatching and wildlife, and a small torch in case of power failures.

Festivals/Public Holidays

January

New Year's Day

Official start of Cricket, Netball and Volleyball Seasons

February

Ash Wednesday (date varies)

March/April

Good Friday (date varies)
Easter Monday *(date varies)

Laser Open Competition – Antigua Yacht Club

International Sailing Week
(runs into May)

Antigua Classic Yacht Regatta
(runs into May)

International Kite Festival

May

Labour Day
(first Monday)

International Sailing Week

Lord Nelson's Ball

Annual Tennis Championships

June

Whit Monday

Antigua and Barbuda Sports Fishing Tournament at Catamaran Club, Falmouth Harbour

July

Official start of Football Season

Caricom Day (first Monday)

Midsummer Carnival
(runs into August)

Wadadl Day Cultural extravaganza

August

Mid-summer Carnival
(first Monday and Tuesday in August are the final days of Carnival)

October

Heritage Day, St John's

Jolly Harbour Annual Sailing Regatta

November

Independence Day 1 November

Moods of Pan St John's

December

Annual Tennis Championships

Annual Nicholson's Boat Show

Agents Week, English Harbour
25th Christmas Day
26th Boxing Day
New Year's Eve
V.C. Bird Day

Health

There are no serious health problems although visitors should take precautions against the sun, which can ruin your holiday. Injections are not required unless visiting from an infected area. All hotels have doctors either resident or on call, and standards of health care are generally high. There are two hospitals on Antigua, one public and one private clinic, and a small hospital on Barbuda. The nearest recompression chambers are at nearby Saba and in St Thomas.

Hospitals

Antigua

Adelin Medical Centre Ltd
Fort Road ☎ 462-0866

Holberton Hospital
Queen Elizabeth Highway ☎ 462-0251 (main hospital)

Barbuda

Spring View Hospital
☎ 460-0076

While there are several pharmacies, medication can be expensive and, if you are taking medicines on prescription, it is advisable to bring enough for your stay.

Tanning safely

The sun is very strong but sea breezes often disguise just how hot it is. If you are not used to the sun take it carefully for the first two or three days, use a good sun screen with a factor of 15 or higher, and do not sunbathe during the hottest parts of the day. Wear sunglasses and a sun hat. Sunglasses will protect you against the glare, especially strong on the beach, and sun hats will protect your head.

If you spend a lot of time swimming or scuba diving take extra care as you will burn even quicker because of the combination of salt water and sun.

Calamine lotion and preparations containing aloe are both useful in combating sunburn.

Irritating insects

Mosquitoes are not much of a problem on or near the beaches because of onshore winds, but they may well bite you as you enjoy an open-air evening meal. Use a good insect repellent, particularly if you are planning trips inland.

Lemon grass can sometimes be found growing naturally, and a handful of this in your room is also a useful mosquito deterrent.

Sand-flies can be a problem on the beach. Despite their tiny size they can give you a nasty bite. And ants exist, so make sure you check the ground carefully before sitting down, otherwise you might get bitten, and the bites can itch for days.

Note: Drinking water from the tap in hotels and resorts is generally safe although bottled mineral and distilled water are widely available.

Language
The official language spoken is English.

Lost Property
Report lost property as soon as possible to your hotel or the nearest police station.

Nightlife/nightclubs
There is a great choice of entertainment from superb dining to cabaret, and karaoke bars to casinos. Many of the larger hotels and resorts offer live entertainment such as steel bands, combos and dancers, and there are bars, dancing and discos, mostly in and around St John's and English Harbour. You can hear great jazz all over Antigua. And, for something really exciting, experience a night dive. Don't miss the Shirley Heights Jump-up.

There are several discos and night spots in St John's, English Harbour and Jolly Harbour. **Grand Princess Casino**, Jolly Harbour Marina (☎ 462-7775), **King's Casino**, **Royal Casino** and **St James** offers gambling. **Rush**, Jolly Harbour Marina (☎ 562 7874) and **Shirley Heights Lookout** (☎ 460-1785), the latter being a great place to spend Sunday afternoon and evening. **18 Carat** on Market Street is a popular dance club and night bar.

Also check out:

Abracadabra
English Harbour ☎ 460-2701

The Beach
Dickenson Bay ☎ 480-6940

Miller's By The Sea
Fort James, live music – from jazz to calypso – every night.

Other Nightclubs

Cats
Sunset Cover, Runaway Bay
☎ 462-3762

Jackpot
High Street, St John's
☎ 462-2359

Traffic
Independence Avenue, St John's
☎ 462-4216

18 Carat
Church Street, St John's
☎ 562-1858

Personal Insurance and Medical Cover

Make sure you have adequate personal insurance and medical cover. If you need to call out a doctor or have medical treatment, you will probably have to pay for it at the time, so keep all receipts so that you can reclaim on your insurance.

Pharmacies

Alpha Pharmacy
Redcliffe Street, St John's
☎ 462-1112

Reliance Pharmacy
Redcliffe Street, St John's
☎ 462-4646

Benjies Pharmacy
Redcliffe Street, St John's
☎ 480-3900

Super Drug Store
Popstead & Bishopgate St
☎ 460-5018

City Pharmacy
St Mary's Street, St John's
☎ 480-3314

Sysco Pharmacy
Jolly Harbour
☎ 462-5917

Food City Pharmacy
Deepwater Harbour
☎ 462-4808

Woods Pharmacy
St Mary's Street, St John's
☎ 462-9388

Gore's Drug Store
Market Street, St John's
☎ 462-1153

Health Pharmacy
Redcliffe Street, St John's
☎ 462-1255

Piper's Pharmacy
All Saints Road, St John's
☎ 462-0736

Photography

The intensity of the sun can play havoc with your pictures, especially if photographing near water or white sand. Compensate for the brightness, otherwise your photographs will come out overexposed and wishy-washy. The heat can actually damage film, so store reels in a box or bag in the hotel fridge if there is one.

Also remember to protect your camera if on the beach, as a single grain of sand is all it takes to jam the mechanism.

It is very easy to get 'click happy', so be tactful and polite when taking photographs. Many islanders are shy or simply fed up with being photographed.

You will have to decide whether the picture is worth it, but if a person declines to have their photograph taken, don't ignore this. The islanders are a warm and very hospitable people and if you stop and spend some time finding out what they are doing they will usually then allow you to take a photograph.

Police

Police Headquarters is on American Road on the outskirts of St John's and there is a police station on the corner of Newgate and Market Streets, as well as in each parish on the island.

Ports

The main port is St John's although English Harbour is the home of the island's charter fleet.

Post Office

The Post Office is in Long Street, just north of Heritage Quay, St John's. Open Monday to Thursday from 8.15am to 12 noon and from 1pm to 4pm (5pm Friday) ☎ 562-1929. There is also a post office in Woods Centre. Open Monday to Thursday 8.30am to 4.00pm and Friday 8.30 to 5.00pm. ☎ 462-9590

Public Toilets

There are not many public toilets on the island, but bars, restaurants and hotels have private facilities which can usually be used if you ask politely.

Restaurants (see pages 60–63)

There is a remarkably large choice when it comes to eating out on the island. There are the inevitable fast food burger, pizza and fried chicken outlets, beach cafés offering excellent value for money, and elegant upmarket dining rooms, as well as restaurants offering a wide range of ethnic cuisines, from Caribbean cooking to Chinese.

Most accept credit cards and during peak times of the year reservations are recommended. If you come across a restaurant that should have been listed in the guide, or have comments about any of those that are, I would very much like to hear from you. Write to me at Florida Features, 375 Douglas Ave, Suite 1002, Altamonte Springs, FL 32714 USA.

Some restaurants are closed on Saturday for lunch and all day Sunday, but hotel restaurants are open daily and welcome outside guests. The restaurants listed ON PAGES 60 TO 63 are classified by price – $ inexpensive, $$ moderate, $$$ expensive.

Security

There is little serious crime but as anywhere it makes sense not to walk around wearing expensive jewels or flashing large sums of money. Secure your valuables as you should anywhere, and do not leave items unattended on the beach or in an unlocked car. Don't carry around your passport or all your money. Keep them secure in your room or in a hotel safety deposit box. It is also a good idea to have photocopies of the information page of your passport, your air ticket and holiday insurance policy. All will help greatly if the originals are lost.

Service Charges and Taxes

There is a government tax of 8.5 per cent on accommodation and restaurant bills. A 10–15 per cent service charge may also be added to restaurant bills. Menus and tariffs sometimes include these charges, so check to make sure they have not been added again. In shops the price on the label is what you pay.

Shells

Shells are washed up onto the beaches but they should be left for others to enjoy. Live shells may not be taken by collectors.

Shopping

Antigua has excellent duty-free shopping from top name designer clothes, to fine china and crystal, perfumes and jewels, and island goods such as handprints, paintings and spices. Shops are generally open from 8am to 4 or 4.30pm Monday to Friday and on Saturday from 8am to noon. Some still close for lunch between noon and 1pm and many in St John's close at noon on Thursday. The main shopping areas are in St John's, the two most fashionable areas being Heritage Quay and Redcliffe Quay, and both open on Sunday if a cruise ship is in port. It is also worth exploring the many streets inland from the waterfront for their interesting and varied shops. There is also good shopping at Jolly Harbour, and many of the hotels and resorts have their own boutiques and shops.

Best buys include: local hand-crafted goods such as straw weaving, pottery, batik, silk-screened printed fabrics, wood carvings and paintings, and Antigua rum. Duty-free bargains include rings, necklaces, etc, watches, perfumes, crystal, china, fine linen and designer sports clothing and beachwear.

Apart from the specialist shops at Heritage Quay and Redcliffe Quay, the following are among those offering island arts and crafts:

Arty Crafts, Rex Halcyon Cove

Museum Gift Shop, St John's

Harbour Art Gallery, Jolly Harbour

Harbour Hall Gallery, Nonsuch Bay

Industrial Workshop for the Blind, All Saints Road

The Restoration Gift Shop, Nelson's Dockyard

Shirley Heights Lookout Gift Shop

Susie's Hot Sauce, Upper North Street, St John's

Sightseeing and Tours

Sightseeing and island tours by land or sea can be arranged through hotels, tour representatives or one of the many specialist tour companies on the island. These include:

Adventure Antigua
☎ 560-4672 and 727-3261

Alexander Parrish
Thames Street, St John's.
Travel service, tours, transfers, bilingual guides
☎ 462-0638

Antigua Destination Planners Ltd – "Paddles"
Seatons, Antigua
☎ 463-1944

Antigua Seafaris
☎726-4435

Antigua Rainforest Canopy Tour
☎ 562-6363

Caribbean Helicopters
Jolly Harbour Marina
☎ 460-5900

Global Travel and Tours
High Street, St John's and Falmouth
☎ 460-3354

Going Places Travel & Tours
Long Street
☎ 480-1230

Kite Antigua
Jabberwock Beach, Hodges Bay
☎ 727-3983

Kiskidee
☎ 462-4801

Suntours
Long and Thames Streets, St John's.
Tours and transfers, multilingual representatives.
☎ 462-4788

Tropical Adventures
Redcliffe Street, St John's
Four-wheel drive offroad adventure, kayaking and power catamaran cruises.
☎ 480-1225

Tropikelly Trails
Four-wheel-drive, off-road adventure tours.
☎ 461-0383

Sport

Cricket

The game is played at every opportunity and anywhere. You can be driving in the countryside, turn a corner and confront players using the road as a wicket. It is played on the beach using a strip of palm for a bat, and even in the water if the tide is coming in. If the island team or the West Indies is playing, almost all the radios on the island are tuned in for the commentary, and matches always draw capacity crowds with a festive atmosphere and picnics. The cricket season lasts from January to May with matches played between island teams, inter-island sides and international test teams.

For the visitor there is a huge range of sporting opportunities from swimming and scuba diving, to hiking and tennis or having a game of cricket with one of the local teams. There is cycling, sailing, squash and, of course, fishing either from shore or boat. The north and east coasts offer stronger swells for windsurfing and surfing but the seas can sometimes be rough and care is needed, while the west and south coast beaches offer safe swimming.

Most hotels offer a variety of sports and water activities, and dive operators offer all levels of instruction. You can learn what it is all about and progress to advanced level if you have the time.

Walking is great fun and there are lots of trails but have stout, non-slip footwear and take a waterproof. Protect yourself against insects, carry adequate drinking water and keep an eye on the time, because night falls quickly and you don't want to be caught out on the trail after dark.

Cycling

Bikes are a good way of getting around and getting a tan. **Bike Plus** ☎ 462-2453 and **Cycle Krazy** ☎ 462-9253 offer rental facilities.

Fitness Gyms

Many of the main hotels and resorts offer health and fitness facilities. In addition there are:

BBR Sportive

Jolly Harbour with squash floodlit tennis and 82-foot (25m) pool. It is open daily from 8am to 9pm and food and soft drinks are available. ☎ 462-6260

Set Physical

State of the art fitness centre, Woods Centre, open 6am–10pm. ☎ 462-9539

National Fitness Centre

Campside, a ten-minute walk from the middle of St John's (just to warm you up), with weight and fitness training equipment, step and aerobic classes. Open Monday to Friday from 6am to 10am and noon to 8pm, and on Saturday from 9am to 2pm. ☎ 462-3681

Paradise Fitness

Jasmine Court, Friar's Hill Road, gym open seven days a week. Free weight area, weight training machines, professional instructors and private training. Aerobic and step classes for all levels. Lockers, changing rooms, showers and juice bar also available. ☎ 460-5000

St James Club

Mamora Bay, hairdresser, massage and beauty treatments. ☎ 460-5000

Temo Sports

English Harbour, has floodlit tennis plus squash courts and equipment can be rented. There is also a bar on the premises. It is open Monday to Saturday from 7am to 10pm. ☎ 460-1781

Tree House

English Harbour, complete body shop for men and women.
☎ 460-3434

Fishing

Fishing is an island pursuit, and many islanders will fish for hours from quayside walls, from the beach or riverside.

There is year-round world-class deep sea and game fishing for Atlantic blue marlin, skipjack, blackfin and yellowfin tuna, also called allison, which can weigh over 100lbs (45.5kg), wahoo and white marlin, which can weigh more than 100lbs (45.5kg), and the fighting sailfish. Snapper, bonefish, permit, pompano, tarpon, grouper, bonito and barracuda can all be caught close to shore. Around the reefs there is an abundance of grouper, jack crevalle, mutton snapper and yellowtail snapper. Dorado is usually called dolphin (not the mammal but the fish also known as mahi-mahi).

There are many guides and charter boats for rent. Prices vary enormously depending on the vessel, number of lines allowed and facilities offered. Fishing charters are offered by :

Missa Fergie ☎ 462-1440

Nightwing ☎ 460-9578

Obsession ☎ 462-3174

Overdraft ☎ 462-0649

Tito I ☎ 460-1452

Vitamin B ☎ 464-4665

(see under Yachting and boating for further details)

Golf

There are two golf courses – Cedar Valley and Jolly Harbour – on Antigua. **Cedar Valley** is a 6,100-yard (5.6km), 71-par, 18-hole championship course which hosts the annual Antiguan Open tournament each March. There is a pro shop, snack shop and bar ☎ 462-0161.

The newest 6,000-yard (5.5km) 71-par 18-hole Harbour Club course is at **Jolly Harbour**. There is a pro shop and clubhouse ☎ 463-8830. All the courses are open to the public and clubs can be rented.

Barbuda offers the 9-hole course at the **K-Club** ☎ 460-0275.

Hiking

There are some spectacular walks around the coast and inland both on Antigua and Barbuda. It is essential to drink plenty of water and take frequent rests, as the walking may be more tiring than you think, and wear sensible, sturdy footwear.

Horseback Riding and Racing

There are several stables on the island and horseback riding can be arranged through hotels. **Spring Hill Riding Club** is on the road to Rendezvous Bay, and offers instruction from BHS qualified staff. There is a floodlit course, cross-country course and range of ponies and horses to suit all sizes and levels of experience. Full and half-day trips can be arranged taking in beach rides, national parks and forest landscapes. Open from 7.30am Tuesday to Sunday for morning sessions, and from 3.30pm for afternoon rides ☎ 460-7787 and 773 3139.

Horse racing takes place at Cassada Gardens, north-east of St John's and near the airport, on most public holidays.

Hunting

There is seasonal deer hunting on Barbuda. A license is required and can be obtained from the police station in Codrington Village.

Scuba diving

The waters offer some of the best diving in the world and are warm (average temperatures being 80°F, 25°C) and remarkably clear with excellent visibility ranging from 50 to 140 feet (15–43m). The fringe barrier reefs are easily accessible and they teem with different corals and marine life – there are almost 400 species of fish. Many of the reefs and shipwrecks are close to the shore, while there are walls, drop-offs, caves and tunnels to explore in deeper waters. Off the south coast of Antigua fallen rocks have created an area of caves and gulleys which is fascinating to explore. The east coast of Antigua offers good diving for experienced divers but the sea conditions can change quickly, and you should only dive with an experienced dive master.

Barbuda is surrounded by reefs and many wrecks, although large areas are still unexplored.

The best Antigua dive sites listed by the tourist office include:

South-west coast

Cades Reef is an extensive formation stretching for 2 miles (3km) with rich fish life and a wide variety of soft and hard coral. Visibility is generally excellent and waters are smooth. Ideal for both scuba and snorkelling.

The Chimney features a small cave at a depth of 60 feet (18m) with sponge-filled gullies as deep as 80 feet (24m). The Chimney is home to many different species of fish including large parrot fish, eels, lobsters and harmless nurse sharks.

Monk's Head gets its name from the coral formations which have sand in the middle and look like a monk's tonsure. Large stingrays swim in the area and you may spot one of the rare eels that inhabit the reef.

Ariadne Shoal is a long ride, taking almost an hour from most dive shops, but well worth the effort. You can dive down to the reefs at a depth of 50 to 80 feet (15–24m) where there are large fish and lobsters, turtles and nurse sharks.

West coast

Thunderhead is a wreck-strewn reef in shallow waters only a short boat ride out. Most of the reef is in 35 feet (11m) of water, although it slopes away gently and you can explore the hard coral and search for treasure.

The Ridge is a wall dive dropping from 25 feet (7m) to the seabed at 60 feet (18m). The wall is covered in small coral heads which are home to thousands of small fish. Nurse sharks swim in the area and you may see an occasional turtle.

The **Andes** is the wreck of a merchant ship which sank in 1905 and now lies in 20 feet (6m) of water at the mouth of Deep Bay. It is now overgrown with coral and home to thousands of brightly hued fish, including the occasional puffer fish.

North and north-west coasts

Jettias is a dive site over the 310-foot (95m) freighter which sank in 1917 and now lies in just 25 feet (7m) of water, which makes it an easy dive even for inexperienced divers and ideal for underwater photography.

Stingray Bank is appropriately named, and one of the best dive sites around the island when the sea conditions are right and the waters are calm. This is another excellent site for underwater photographers.

South coast

Shirley Heights has many dive sites inshore as the waters drop to a depth of 100 feet (30m). There are coral ledges, walls and drop-offs, and interesting rock formations that are the homes of rays and spade fish and also shelter the occasional turtle.

Sunken Rock is for experienced divers only and begins at a depth of about 40 feet (12m), where there is a coral-encrusted canyon. This can be followed to a sandy ledge, from where the rock face drops quickly to well below 120 feet (37m). Here you can dive among the barracuda, rays and amberjack.

Dive companies and dive schools

Aquanaut Diving Centre

St James's Club, Marmora Bay, offers PADI, NAUI and NASE certification courses.
☎ 460-5000

Rex Halcyon Cove Dive Antigua

Dickenson Bay, offers NAUI courses.
☎ 462-3483

Dockyard Divers

English Harbour
☎ 460-1178.

Jolly Dive

Club Antigua, Jolly Harbour
☎ 462-8305

Long Bay Dive Shop

Long Bay ☎ 463-2005

Jumby Bay

Offer dive packages. ☎ 462-6000

Indigo Divers

Jolly Harbour
☎ 729-3483

Snorkelling

Many reefs lie close to the shore and are easily accessible. Glass-bottom boats and other charter vessels go to deeper reefs where you can snorkel. The following offer snorkelling trips:

Aquanaut
☎ 460-5000

Long Bay Dive Shop
☎ 463-2005

Dockyard Divers
☎ 460-1178

Miguel's Holiday Adventure
☎ 460-9978/723-5826

Dive Antigua
☎ 462-3483

Sentio
☎ 464-7127

Jolly Dive
☎ 462-8305

Wadadli Cats
☎ 462-4792

Kokomo Cat
☎ 462-7245

Squash

There are facilities at **BBR Sportive** at Jolly Harbour ☎ 462-6260 and **Temo Sports** in English Harbour ☎ 460-1781.

Tennis

The Annual Tennis Championships are held in January, May and December and attract top-ranking US and European players.

There are many courts on all the islands, some floodlit, and many hotels offer tennis packages which include court time and coaching. Some of the larger hotels also host annual tennis tournaments. Not all hotel courts are open to the public.

If newly arrived on the island, book a court early in the morning or late in the afternoon when it is cooler until you get used to the heat.

Watersports and aquatic activities

These are available at all resorts and most large hotels and range from Hobie Cats, jet skis, windsurfers, kayaks and sunfish. Experts are also on hand to teach you how to sail, waterski and parasail. Waterskiers must always operate well away from swimmers. There is excellent windsurfing on Antigua and Barbuda because of the year-round onshore trade winds. There are beginners' schools on the more sheltered west coast, while intermediate and experienced windsurfers can enjoy the Atlantic rollers on the east coast. Galley Bay and Turtle Bay offer the best year-round surfing.

Halcyon Cove Watersports

Waterskiing and small boats for rent. ☎ 462-0256.

Jolly Harbour Watersports

Jolly Harbour ☎ 462-7979. Situated on this startling long, white beach, right next to Castaways Beach Bar. Offers a wide variety of watersports and activities.

Kite Antigua

Learn to kite sail on the north coast of Antigua at Jabberwock Beach. For beginners to advanced. Open daily from 8.30am. ☎ 727-3983.

Sunsail Club Colonna

Hodges Bay ☎ 462-6263. One of the largest watersports centres in the Caribbean with a huge choice of watersport activities.

Yachting and boating, marinas and berthing facilities

The offshore waters are a Mecca for yachtsmen from around the world. English Harbour is the main base for the island's famous yacht charter fleet.

International Sailing Week takes place at the end of April and beginning of May. It is the premier regatta in the Caribbean and one of the top five in the world. The annual regatta attracts entries from throughout the Caribbean, Europe, and North and South America. Apart from the yacht races, this is the time for great beach parties and meeting people, culminating in the award ceremony at the Lord Nelson's Ball held at the Admiral's Inn, English Harbour.

Yacht charters

Nicholson's Yacht Charters, Nelson's Dockyard ☎ 460-1530
Sun Yacht Charters, Nelson's Dockyard ☎ 460-2615

Marinas

Antigua Slipway, Nelson's Dockyard, English Harbour ☎ 460-1056
Antigua Yacht Club and Marina, Falmouth Harbour ☎ 460-1444
Catamaran Hotel and Marina, Falmouth Harbour ☎ 460-1036
Jolly Harbour Marino, Jolly Harbour ☎ 462-6041
St James's Yacht Club, Mamora Bay ☎ 460-5000

Cruises and water sightseeing trips

There are tours aboard glass-bottomed boats to the many nature islands off Antigua, and these offer an excellent way of viewing the rich marine life and coral reefs.

Horatio Historic Cruises

Operates 30-minute cruises around Nelson's Dockyard. They run daily every 30 minutes from 10am to 5pm ☎ 460-1178.

Eli's Eco Tours

Offers small groups an inside look at the hidden islands, reefs and waterways of the North Sound. These tours have themes of history and ecology. Snorkelling, caving, hiking and exploring the mangrove habitats are part of this full-day tour. ☎ 560-4672 and 727 3261.

Excellence

Sail aboard this high-speed power catamaran which will take you around Antigua or across to Barbuda with its fascinating frigate bird colony or to Montserrat to view the active volcano. Discover the secrets of these islands in the luxury of *Excellence*. ☎ 480-1225.

Black Swan Pirate Party Cruises

Fun cruises daily with wining, dining and dancing, swimming and snorkelling. ☎ 562-7946.

Kokomo Cat Cruises

A 61-foot (18m) catamaran – *Kokomo* – sails to nearby islands and secluded beaches for snorkelling and picnics, as well as running sunset cruises. ☎ 462-7245.

Miguel's Holiday Adventure

Sails from Hodges Bay on Tuesday, Thursday and Saturday at 10am for the five-minute crossing to Prickly Pear Island, where the day can be spent on the beach fishing, swimming, snorkelling and picnicking. All equipment is included. The boat returns at 4pm. Special trips can be arranged. ☎ 461-0361.

Obsession

A 45-foot (14m) Hatteras sport fishing boat equipped to the highest specifications, and offering deep sea fishing and sightseeing trips. It sails from the Falmouth Harbour marina. ☎ 462-3174.

Paradise I

A French-built 45-foot (14m) sailing yacht that can accommodate up to 14 people. It offers full-day sailing cruises including lunch and open bar, and is also available for charter. ☎ 462-4158.

Sea Sports

Dickenson Bay. ☎ 462-3355.

Sentio

A 45-foot (14m) luxury sailing ketch ideal for small groups, honeymooners and special occasions. It sails to secluded beaches for picnics and snorkelling, and also offers half and full day cruises, learn-to-sail cruises, sunset and overnight trips to Barbuda. ☎ 464-7127.

Shorty's Glass Bottom Boat

Offers two cruises daily from Dickenson Bay to the offshore reefs.

Tito

A powerful 34-foot (10m) Scarab Supersport with twin engines, offering day tours to nearby islands and remote beaches for swimming, picnicking and snorkelling. Deep sea fishing charters are also available. ☎ 460-3336.

Treasure Island Cruises

Cruise to the music of a steel band with full buffet, open bar, limbo and lots of fun. ☎ 461-8698.

Wadaldi Cats

Four well-established catamarans that take you around Antigua to visit and explore the most deserted coves and beaches. Freshwater showers, convenient stem ladders and a large roofed area – all for your comfort. Bar and barbecue pit on board. The latest addition to the fleet is the *Spirit of Excellence*, which guarantees the fastest speeds, taking you quickly to your destination. All catamarans are available for private charter, sunset cruises, Barbuda day trips – you can design your own itinerary ☎ 462-4792.

Taxis

Antigua Taxi Stand, Market Street	☎ 462-0711
Brothers, Lower Long Street, St John's	☎ 462-6464
Christo, High Street, St John's	☎ 460-7434
Heritage Quay Taxi Stand, St John's	☎ 562-0280
Ivor Taxi, Liberta Village	☎ 460-3357
Sandals Antigua Taxi Stand	☎ 462-0267
Twenty Four Hours Taxi Stand	☎ 460-5353
West Bus Station Taxis, St John's	☎ 462-5190

Telephones

International communications on the island are provided by Cable and Wireless, whose main office is on Long Street, St John's ☎ 480-4234. There is also a sub office in Nelson's Dockyard ☎ 480-2626.

The international code for Antigua is 268. From the US dial 1-268 and the seven-digit island number. Direct calling is available to and from most countries. From the UK and Europe dial 001-268 and the seven-digit island number. To ring the US from Antigua dial 1 + area code + seven-digit local number. To use AT&T Direct dial 1-800-872-2881 or #1. To ring the UK from Antigua dial 011-44-area code+seven-digit local number. For credit card calls dial 1-800-877-8000. Cellular phones can be rented through Cable & Wireless (Caribbean Cellular), ☎ 480-2628 and APUA PCS, ☎ 727-2782 if you want to stay in touch or are planning to cruise for a few days. Many establishments can also be contacted by radio phone on one of the VHF Channels.

Time

Antigua operates under Eastern Standard Time, and Eastern Daylight Time between April and October. During the winter Antigua is four hours behind London and during the summer five hours.

Tipping

Tips are generally added to restaurant bills but check in case they are not, in which case add 10–15 per cent. It is customary to tip bellboys in hotels, taxi drivers, guides and other people providing a service. Tip taxi drivers around 10–15 per cent and bellboys $1 for each piece of luggage.

Tourist Offices

There are Tourist Information Centres at the VC Bird International Airport. The **Antigua and Barbuda Tourist Office** is at: Government Complex, Queen Elizabeth Highway, St John's.
☎ 268-462-0480 Fax 268-2483.

Overseas Tourist Offices

US

New York, 305 East 47th Street, Suite 6a, New York, NY 10017

25 SE 3ND Avenue, Suite 3
Miami, Florida FL 33131
☎ 305-381-6762

3216 New Mexico Avenue,
N. W., Washington D C 20016
☎ 202-362-5122

Canada

60 St Clair Avenue East, Suite 601 Toronto, Ontario M4T 1N5 ☎ 416-961-3085

France

43 Avenue de Friedland, Paris 75008
☎ 1-53-75-15-71

Italy

Via Santa Maria, Alla Porta 9, 20123
Milan, Italy ☎ 039-02-877983

UK

2nd floor, 45 Crawford Place, London, WIH 4LP
☎ 011-44-207-528-0070

Germany

Thomas strasse 11. D-61348 Bad Homburg ☎ 49-6172-21504

Weddings

Antigua is becoming an increasingly popular destination for honeymoon couples, and other couples get carried away by the romance of the island and decide to marry while on vacation. If you decide to marry you can enjoy a traditional church ceremony or make your vows on the beach, on a luxury yacht or in a flower-bedecked gazebo by a sparkling hotel pool.

To qualify for a special licence you must:
• have a valid passport or birth certificate and ID photo;
• if either party is single, an affidavit must be sworn on Antigua or Barbuda to that affect and that they are free to marry;
• if either party is divorced, a certified copy of the decree absolute must be shown;
• if either party were married and the marriage ended with the death of their partner, a copy of both the marriage and death certificates must be produced;
• if either party is under the age of 18, parental or guardian consent is required. You must be over 15 years old to get married.

There is no waiting time in the country necessary in order to obtain a special licence, but both parties must be present at the time of the application, which is filled out and signed at the Ministry of Justice and Legal Affairs in Lower Nevis Street, St John's. The ministry is open Monday to Thursday 8.30am to 4.30pm and Friday 8am to 3pm. The petition for a special licence costs US$150. There is a US$40 fee to register and the marriage officer's fee is US$50. An ordinary licence costs EC$100 and all the above conditions must be met. In addition, one of the parties must have been resident in Antigua or Barbuda for at least 15 days before applying for the licence. All marriages must be celebrated in the presence of two or more credible witnesses in addition to the Marriage Officer or Registrar General. Marriage by licence can take place anywhere within Antigua and Barbuda providing all the formalities have been complied with and the arrangements accepted by the Registrar General.

Many hotels and resorts offer weddings and honeymoon packages, and have staff experienced in helping with all the formalities and arrangements.

The Registrar General's office is on Queen Elizabeth Highway ☎ 462-0609/0409/3929.

And for the Honeymoon...

A number of hotels offer specially designed honeymoon packages.

The Admiral's Inn
Nelson's Dockyard, English Harbour,
Antigua ☎ 460-1027

Allegro Resort
Long Bay, Antigua ☎ 463-2006

Antigua Village
Dickenson Bay ☎ 462-2930

Beach Comber Hotel
Winthrops Bay ☎ 462-3100

Blue Waters Beach Hotel
Soldier's Bay, Antigua ☎ 462-0290

Cocobay
Valley Church ☎ 562-2400

Coco Point
Barbuda ☎ 462 3816

Copper and Lumber Store Hotel
Nelson's Dockyard ☎ 460-1058

Curtain Bluff Old Road
Morris Bay, ☎ 462 8400

Galleon Beach Club
English Harbour ☎ 460-1024

Galley Bay Hotel
Five Islands, Antigua ☎ 462-0302

Harmony Hall
Nonsuch Bay ☎ 460 4120

Hawksbill Beach Hotel
Five islands, Antigua ☎ 462-0301

Inn at English Harbour
English Harbour ☎ 460-1014

Jolly Beach Resort
Lignumvitae Bay ☎ 462-0061

Jolly Harbour Villas
Jolly Harbour ☎ 462-3085

Pineapple Beach Club
Grand Long Bay, Antigua ☎ 463-2006

Rex Halcyon Cove
Dickenson Bay ☎ 462-0256

Sandals Antigua
Dickenson Bay, Antigua
☎ 462-0267

Siboney Beach Club
Dickenson Bay ☎ 462-0806

St James Club
Marmora Bay, Antigua ☎ 460-5000

Index

Published in the UK by
Landmark Publishing Ltd
Ashbourne Hall, Cokayne Ave, Ashbourne, Derbyshire DE6 1EJ England
Tel: 01335 347349 Fax: 01335 347303
e-mail: landmark@clara.net website: landmarkpublishing.co.uk

Published in the USA by
Hunter Publishing Inc
222 Clematis Street, West Palm Beach, FL 33401, USA
Website: www.hunterpublishing.com

3rd Edition
ISBN 13: 978-1-84306-368-1

British Library Cataloguing in Publication Data: a catalogue record for this book is available from the British Library.

Printed by: Gutenberg Press, Malta

Designed by: Michelle Hunt

Edited by: Ian Howe

Front Cover: The gorgeous crystal clear, turquoise waters and lush, green landscape of Antigua and Barbuda set the stage for romance. (Photo Credit: Antigua and Barbuda Ministry of Tourism)

Back cover, top: Antigua and Barbuda offers travelers many exciting adventures to choose from. (Photo Credit: Antigua and Barbuda Ministry of Tourism)

Back cover, middle: Visitors to Antigua can enjoy a breathtaking, panoramic view of English Harbour from the hilltop of Shirley Heights. (Photo Credit: Antigua and Barbuda Ministry of Tourism)

Back cover, bottom: A visit to the laid-back Caribbean islands of Antigua and Barbuda doesn't mean cutting back on luxury. Antigua and Barbuda's accommodations range from luxe all-inclusive resorts and spacious villas, to historic inns and intimate beachfront apartments. (Photo Credit: Caribrep Villas Antigua)